A Guide To Web Marketing

SUCCESSFUL PROMOTION ON THE NET

JUDY DAVIS

IN ASSOCIATION WITH
Marketing MAGAZINE

KOGAN
PAGE

I am very grateful to all those who contributed material for this book. Special thanks to Marc de Swaan Arons (Marketing Director of Unilever's Interactive Brand Centre) and to Graham Wood (Lecturer in International Marketing and Marketing Communications at Leeds Metropolitan University) for their input and advice.

First published in 2000

Kogan Page Limited
120 Pentonville Road
London
N1 9JN
UK

Kogan Page Limited
163 Central Avenue, Suite 2
Dover
NH 03820
USA

British Library Cataloguing in Publication Data

A CIP record for this book is available from the British Library.

ISBN 0 7494 3185 7

Typeset by Jean Cussons Typesetting, Diss, Norfolk
Printed and bound in Great Britain by Clays Ltd, St Ives plc

Contents

Introduction

Internet fever has gripped the commercial world. Every day comes news of more businesses going online, companies offering free access to the Internet, start-up ventures opening up new market opportunities, technological advances and new advertising possibilities. The stock market frenzy for Internet companies has made fortunes for the early pioneers of the Web, and yet few companies are actually making a profit.

The Internet may be surrounded by media hype and shrouded in technical jargon, but it is difficult to ignore its pervasive influence. The *digital* revolution will eventually affect every aspect of daily life, even if it does not happen quite as fast as enthusiasts would have us believe. The way in which we communicate, organize both work and private lives, shop, bank, find entertainment and relaxation will all be influenced by the new media, the most significant of which is the Internet.

Marketers need to get to grips with this trend in order to stay in touch with the needs of their customers and consumers. Those who fail to do so run the risk of losing ground to their competitors. Nor is it enough to delegate responsibility for developing a Web campaign to the IT department: they may have the technical know-how but have little marketing experience.

The good news is that deep technical knowledge is not vital in order to assess the commercial implications of the World Wide Web and to work out how it can be exploited to develop the business.

THE INTERNET MARKETING PROCESS

Marketers need to arm themselves with an overview of the opportunities and limitations of the new technology, have a grasp of the marketing issues, and then apply basic marketing principles.

Explore the market opportunity

The World Wide Web can be exploited in many ways: for communication and entertainment, as a new channel of distribution, for business-to-business or business-to-consumer purposes. The challenge for commercial ventures on the Web is how to do so profitably... both in the short and long term.

Review competitor activity

New business models are emerging as electronic commerce rapidly gains acceptance. The relatively low cost of entry to the Web makes it an ideal place for entrepreneurial start-up businesses. The rules are changing and new sources of competition may challenge traditional businesses. Even those who do not intend to use the Web as part of their marketing strategy may need to adapt their way of doing business in response to competitors on the Web.

Understand the target consumer

Internet usage is no longer confined to geeks and anoraks, and nearly half of all users are women. Users no longer just surf for 'cool' sites, but expect to find something useful. However, different consumer groups have different needs and expectations, ranging from the convenience of online transactions, through the reassurance of product information, to the thrill of games and chat lines.

Define the user benefit

This should meet a user need, and be offered in a way that other media cannot deliver. Interactivity is important. Product information, customized products and services, low prices and the convenience of direct sales may attract consumers, particularly where the product is of high value and high interest. Low interest products need to offer added value in the form of utility, education or entertainment.

Set objectives

The Web offers a great opportunity for one-to-one communication with customers and consumers, and even if direct selling is not an option, a relationship can be built up and loyalty generated. But not every brand or business can expect to strike up a meaningful one-to-one relationship with busy users, who have a life beyond the Internet. Objectives should be realistic in the context of the product offered. For maximum effect Web activity should be an integral part of the brand strategy: synergies can be found with other media only if the objectives and communication message are consistent.

Define roles and responsibilities

Sales and marketing should take responsibility for setting objectives, and work with the IT department to find solutions and ensure that adequate resources are made available. Interactive media such as the Web require specialist knowledge, and it may be necessary to review the skills and experience within the organization and house agencies. New media specialists and consultants abound, and it may be better to outsource creative work as well as technical implementation.

Consider the options

Depending on the objectives, a Web presence can be established in a number of ways: launching and maintaining a Web site; advertising on sites already frequented by the target market; and sponsoring content. The choice of route has implications for resources, and it is important to consider the organizational implications of embarking on a Web campaign.

Brief design and creative work

The Web is essentially an interactive medium requiring very different creative solutions to traditional media. Advertising, promotions and online sales must all reflect the dynamic Web

environment and users' high expectations of an interactive experience. But as custodians of communication consistency, marketers
must avoid getting so carried away by the possibilities of the
medium that they lose sight of the objectives.

Set up systems for e-commerce

Not every Web site needs to conduct transactions, but increasingly
merchants are seeking to sell online direct to the consumer. This
gives rise to a lot of additional complexity such as secure payments
and integration with existing systems, and potentially raises
currency and pricing issues.

Check legal issues

The Internet retains much of its original anarchic culture, where
freedom of information, anonymity and creativity prevail. There is
no central regulatory body, and protection of trademarks and
personal data, pricing transparency and copyright piracy are hot
issues. It is advisable to take some basic legal precautions and be
aware of the possible issues.

Measure quantified targets

Although Web spin doctors praise the accountability of the
medium, there are barriers to accurate consumer targeting and
many different ways to measure Web traffic. Talk of 'hits' and
'impressions' are meaningless unless everybody uses the same
definitions, and increasing frustration from advertisers is putting
pressure on the industry to agree common standards of audience
measurement and advertising practices. Until this happens, direct
comparisons with other media may be difficult to make.

Conduct market research

Not all objectives can be quantified, and reasons for using the Web
as part of the marketing programme may have more to do with
building a long-term presence than achieving short-term targets.
Research can be used to gain experience of how consumers use the
Web and to learn how it can benefit the business in the future.

The Internet marketing process is summarized in Figure 0.1.

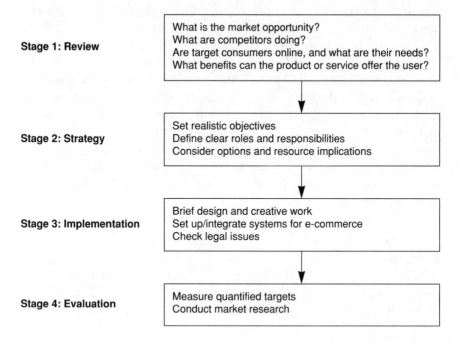

Stage 1: Review

What is the market opportunity?
What are competitors doing?
Are target consumers online, and what are their needs?
What benefits can the product or service offer the user?

Stage 2: Strategy

Set realistic objectives
Define clear roles and responsibilities
Consider options and resource implications

Stage 3: Implementation

Brief design and creative work
Set up/integrate systems for e-commerce
Check legal issues

Stage 4: Evaluation

Measure quantified targets
Conduct market research

Figure 0.1   *Summary of the Internet marketing process*

ABOUT THIS BOOK

A Guide to Web Marketing goes through each stage of the process outlined in Figure 0.1, providing readers with background information, strategic insights and practical tips for integrating the Web into their marketing plan. At the end of each chapter, there is a brief explanation of technical terms and jargon that appear in italics in the text, and a full Glossary is provided at the end of the book. Case studies and examples illustrate key points in 'real life', with reference to over 100 Web sites. The checklist at the end of each chapter aims to help users identify their individual business needs and draw up appropriate action plans. At the end of the book there is, in addition to the Glossary, an index to the Web sites mentioned in the text and a list of useful contacts and further reading.

Chapter glossary

Digital   Digital information works on a single stream of ones and zeros, electrical positives and negatives, or pulses and lack-of-pulses. It has now become possible to convert into digits information that would once have been transmitted in analogue waves, such as music, speech and moving pictures. Information that is handled digitally does not need a special machine for each task; it can be sent from one computer to another, from a computer to the set-top box of a television, or to a mobile telephone. The same service can be delivered to the home or office by telephone line, cable or satellite. This opens up a proliferation of communication possibilities, blurring the traditional distinctions between media.

1

The Internet: A New Medium

The Internet is probably the most exciting and talked-about new medium since television. Its interactive capabilities offer enormous potential. The challenge for marketing is deciding how best to exploit this potential in the pursuit of commercial objectives, and to integrate a new medium into the marketing mix.

FROM SCIENTIFIC/ACADEMIC USE TO COMMERCIAL MEDIUM

In the 1980s and early 1990s scientists, academics, computer experts and students dominated the Internet. It was first developed in 1969 when the US government decided to connect some of its computers together to enable scientists and military agencies to communicate more easily. Due to the knowledge and skills required, use of the Internet was initially limited to the scientific and academic world.

The development of user-friendly software and the growth in penetration of personal computers in the 1990s have encouraged a far wider range of people to use the Internet. Developments in digital technology will in time allow the Internet to be delivered through means other than personal computers. It will soon be possible to access the Internet from televisions equipped with a set-top box and from mobile phones, making it available to many more people.

An *Internet service provider* (ISP) connects an individual's personal computer to the Internet where it can communicate with other computers. The original ISPs (such as start-up business Demon Internet) charge a monthly subscription fee to cover access to cyberspace and services including a telephone help-line. In addition to the flat monthly fee, the user pays the telephone bill for time connected to the Internet. America Online (AOL) is one of the world's most popular paid-for ISPs, and in addition to Internet access it offers its subscribers huge amounts of content (including news, sport, weather and hundreds of chat rooms), and a selection of shopping services.

The emergence of companies prepared to offer access to the Internet free of charge has led to a massive increase in the number of Internet users in the UK in 1999. The successful launch and flotation of Dixons' Freeserve, which charges no subscription fees but shares the revenues generated by calls to their Internet service with the telephone company, has inspired a number of leading high-street brands to set up their own free ISPs. It is estimated there were over 200 free ISPs in the UK by August 1999. As the focus of charges shifts from subscriptions to calls, analysts predict that new services offering free local calls are likely to emerge.

This sudden rush to provide free services is not motivated by altruism but rather by the prospect of future commercial gain. The recognition that the Internet is a new medium that will have a significant impact on society is attracting entrepreneurs and businesses. They are willing to invest huge sums of money today – or afraid not to – in the hope of shaping the development of the Internet from free information channel to commercial medium. And the first step is to build a customer base.

GROWTH OF THE WORLD WIDE WEB

The *World Wide Web* is the fastest growing and commercially most important part of the Internet. Exponential growth worldwide is predicted over the next few years, although some of this is hype from interested industry parties.

The Web is a highly versatile system used for publishing and browsing through a complex web of text, graphics, images, audio and video. Accessed via a browser, it offers:

▓ a vast quantity of data and intellectual property available to be copied and downloaded;
▓ the possibility of developing relationships between people, organizations and 'communities of interest' through *chat* and interactive services;
▓ the opportunity to explore the Web for information on specific areas of interest, buy products or services, search for career opportunities, play games, or just generally 'surf' to see what is out there.

The Web has infinite capacity and the supply of material continues to grow rapidly. At the end of 1999 there were 8 million sites to choose from, offering something for everyone, from rocket scientist to Bengali cat lover. However, a common complaint about the Web is that it is mind-boggling and overloaded with information – the resource in short supply is people's time and attention in a busy world. Just because a new medium exists does not mean that people necessarily want it. Consumer demand is dependent on the quality and utility of the material provided and the way in which it is published.

Growth is currently inhibited by limited *bandwidth*, and the inability to deliver full video and real-time interactivity through existing communication links. Many *information superhighways* are overloaded with traffic because there is insufficient bandwidth, making *download* time frustratingly slow and earning the Web its nickname the 'World Wide Wait'. *E-commerce* (electronic commerce) needs *backbone* networks with enough bandwidth to support leading edge services in order to compete effectively.

Capacity can be increased in a number of ways, for example by *data compression*, *fibre-optic cables*, adapting cable-television networks and using combinations of satellite and telephone. In the US, 1998 saw improved bandwidth delivery to the home through cable TV and other digital line upgrades, but Europe has more problems with getting access at reasonable cost to the type of bandwidth required for digital services, paying up to ten times more than in the US.

A new technology called Asymmetrical Digital Subscriber Line (*ADSL*) is being developed, and this promises much faster access to the Internet and better pictures and movies. However, this type of *broadband* delivery is more expensive than conventional narrow-band, and it is unlikely that anybody will give it away free, including ISPs such as Freeserve.

ENTERTAINMENT MEDIUM, SOURCE OF INFORMATION AND DISTRIBUTION CHANNEL

The Internet is probably the first genuinely new medium in a generation, and its possibilities are still being explored. There are different visions of its potential: as an entertainment medium like the television, as a convenient means of communicating and retrieving information like the telephone, and as a new distribution channel.

An entertainment medium

In the early days, many US companies saw the emerging World Wide Web as the new mass entertainment medium for the next century. Soon computer screens were serving up a crude version of 'interactive television': online soap operas and TV guides, online interviews with prime time stars, 'Webzines' on pop culture and music, even text-based soap operas.

But the industry's vision for the medium ran ahead of technological capabilities. The personal computer combined with limited bandwidth are unsatisfactory for downloading still images from the Web, let alone the full-motion video and sound that consumers expect. Downloading video and music on the Web has been compared with pulling an elephant through a straw. *Cyberspace* is littered with the bodies of aborted entertainment ventures as profits and viewers failed to match up to the other entertainment media. In 1998, AOL cut staff in its entertainment division, and the Microsoft network reduced its entertainment focus.

The Internet is still in its infancy. In the next few years, consumers will get faster links on the Web via upgraded phone lines, wireless and satellite links and superfast modems hooked to cable-TV wires. As graphics, video and sound improve, multimedia in the home may become commonplace. Paramount, Disney and MGM are all exploring the entertainment possibilities of the Internet.

The future of entertainment on the Web now lies largely with online games, which attract an increasingly mainstream audience and commercial interest. Sega's Dreamcast console is being sold on its online capabilities, and a raft of new Web-based real-life war games, fantasy role-playing and family games are expected to be launched in 2000.

A source of information

The Internet may yet prove to be as revolutionary as the development of the printing press as an information distribution system. Unlimited information can be posted on the Internet, and delivered at minimal cost. One of the Internet's strengths is as a 'telephone book', able to help consumers find the right needle in a digital haystack of data.

News, stock quotes and sports scores are among the most popular categories of online content. At Time Warner's Pathfinder site (www.pathfinder.com), news information has grown much faster than entertainment. The *Financial Times* offers up-to-date news stories, stock market information updated every 15 minutes, and a global news archive (www.ft.com).

The Web is widely used for research and educational purposes, and for searching for career and job opportunities. It provides practical services such as *electronic mail*, telephone and business directories, used car price guides, and maps with driving directions. UK surfers go through more than 1 million pages weekly of British Telecom's Yellow Pages site (www.yell.co.uk).

Advertisers are increasingly attracted by the Web's ability to deliver product information and promotional messages to a tightly defined audience. Unlike mass media where a common message is delivered to everyone, the Web allows information to be customized to meet the needs of individuals, and a one-to-one relationship to be built.

A new channel of distribution

The Internet provides a global, 24-hour channel for conducting electronic commerce for companies that embrace Web technology.

This can be either a source of incremental sales, often achieved with little increase in fixed costs, or a new venture. Entrepreneurs may find a way to break in to existing markets to sell direct to the consumer, or create new market segments through innovative thinking.

E-commerce is already significant in selling holidays, property, books and CDs. The music industry is now looking seriously at the Web as a distribution outlet. Online retailer Musicmaker (www.musicmaker.com) already sells CDs over the Web, allowing people to compile personalized discs from favourite tracks on EMI's back catalogue, and download them on to CDs at their local shop. Pop stars are signing up to put music out on MP3.com (www.mp3.com), the most popular *MP3* site, and some pundits predict that in five years' time, 50 per cent of the singles chart will be downloaded from the Web.

BUSINESS-TO-BUSINESS

Online retailing to consumers is just the tip of the e-commerce iceberg: the Internet can potentially enhance every stage of a company's activities. The 'value chain' model of primary and support activities linked to create value, gain competitive advantage and generate margin can be adapted to illustrate this; see Figure 1.1.

Electronic commerce is already relatively well established in a business-to-business context, not least because the majority of commercial operations are already hooked up to the Internet. Many business-to-business transactions are conducted through semi-private *intranets* and *extranets*, which link companies with their suppliers. This has transformed supply chain management and inventory control. Intranet and extranet links can be used throughout the value chain in a variety of different ways, to improve efficiency and communication. For example, product drawings, designs and blueprints can be transferred electronically from a designer to his or her clients and to production facilities.

The World Wide Web also simplifies the procurement process. Web sites that serve as online sales brochures may facilitate research for both technology development and purchasing by providing access to the latest product information from suppliers

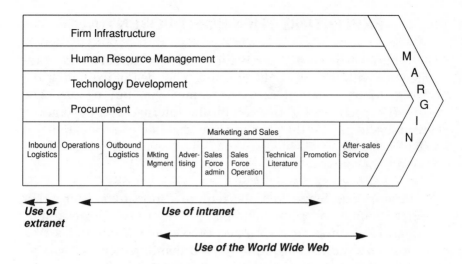

Figure 1.1   *The Internet and the value chain*

Adapted with the permission of The Free Press, a division of Simon & Schuster, from *Competitive Advantage: Creating and sustaining superior performance* by Michael E Porter, © 1985, 1998 Michael E Porter.

and component makers. Secure 'meeting rooms' can even be set up on a company Web site. For example, a design agency may allocate client companies a private meeting room where they can use a password to access plans and drawings relating to a particular project.

A Web site can offer several advantages at the same time. For example, Wedgwood's Web site promotes the range to consumers, sells to smaller retailers, and provides cost savings through improved efficiency. Individual customers use the Web site (www.wedgwood.com) to find out about the product range, while retail distributors can use it to place and track orders. As a result, in addition to boosting sales:

▓ order accuracy is improved, since customers key requests directly into the order entry system;

▓ communication with retailers is improved through the use of e-mail;

▓ customers can check what's happening to their order at any time of the day or night.

EXPLOITING THE PROFIT POTENTIAL

The Internet was started for non-commercial military and academic uses with little thought of profit. The idea of exploiting the Internet for commercial purposes came later. But people have come to expect free information on the Internet, and persuading consumers to pay for the privilege of using online services remains a challenge. Internet businesses can seek to generate revenue from a number of sources:

▨ Subscriptions. Some Web sites require visitors to register, either in exchange for personal data, or for a fee. For example, financial services firm Dun and Bradstreet Corporation's Web sites (www.dnb.com and www.dunandbrad.co.uk) charge subscribers per report for credit reports on businesses. A common tactic adopted by services such as online news is to offer free access initially to attract trial, and then once sufficient users have been recruited to impose a subscription fee in the hope that the fall-out rate will not be too high.

▨ Online sales, or sales commission. Online retailers such as Amazon (www.amazon.com and www.amazon.co.uk) offer books, CDs and other goods for sale via their own Web site. ISPs and other content sites provide merchants with the opportunity to trade from their Web sites in return for a flat fee, or a cut of all transactions.

▨ Selling advertising space. For example, Amazon earns revenue not only from selling books online but also from selling advertising space on its own Web site.

▨ Royalties on advertisers' sales. For example, Amazon pays to advertise on the AOL site, and also pays them a royalty on books sold through the advertisement.

▨ Licensing a service to other Web sites. For example, GeoSystems' Mapquest site (www.mapquest.com) attracts more than 5 million visitors a month for free custom-made maps (worldwide) and a route planning service (US only), and licenses the service to other business sites.

▨ Cost savings. Fedex receives 1.7 million package-tracking requests a month over the Internet: the company estimates 40 per cent of its traffic would otherwise dial their free phone number to do the same thing, and handling each call typically costs about US $1. The Web site thus saves Fedex up to US $8 million a year in customer-support costs.

■ Revenue-sharing arrangements. ISPs World Online and Freeserve share the revenue generated from telephone minutes online with the telecommunications companies.

INTERNET FEVER

Company results to date for Internet-based enterprises are mixed. While some sites are achieving profits, many others are struggling to survive their *'burn rate'* – the money a company spends each month exceeding its revenues. Despite the lack of short-term profit the US stock market is wildly bullish about Internet companies, as the comparison of market worth and estimated earnings, in Table 1.1, shows. Enthusiasm for Internet stock was also a feature of the UK market in 1999.

Table 1.1 *Valuation of Internet companies*

Top Internet companies	Market worth Nov. 1998 $m	Estimated earnings 1998 $m
America Online	38,435	255.0
Yahoo!	19,229	49.2
Amazon.com	7,276	–90.6
@Home	5,592	–52.0
Ebay	4,990	5.2
Sterling Com	3,064	97.0
Inktomi	2,920	–118.3
Netscape Com	2,852	52.3
Lycos	2,193	–3.4
Excite	2,304	–42.0

Freeserve
www.freeserve.com, www.freeserve.net, www.freeserve.co.uk, www.freeserve.org

Freeserve, electrical retailer Dixons' free Internet Service Provider, reflects the City's current enthusiasm for all Internet stocks. The 1999 flotation was 30 times over-subscribed, and valued the business at over £2 billion – as much as well-established high-street brands such as Next or Thomson Travel. This valuation was based on future expectations rather than current earnings: by May 1999, after eight months of operation, Freeserve had generated revenue of £2.73 million and made net losses of £1.04 million.

Freeserve offers more than just free access to the World Wide Web: it also delivers a search engine, UK-focused content, and e-commerce opportunities with online merchants trading over the site. Unlike ISPs such as AOL, Freeserve does not charge subscription fees for providing Internet access. Instead it shares the revenues generated by calls to its Internet service with Energis, the telephone company. However, it is anticipated that this source of revenue will decline as the industry comes under pressure to offer cheaper or even free local calls.

But the most important factor is the size – and quality – of the user base. By the end of 1999, Freeserve had built up the UK's largest registered user base, with 1.48 million subscribers. As the number of Internet users mushrooms, with penetration in Britain reaching an expected 40 per cent of the population by 2002, it is predicted that this will lead to an advertising boom, and a sharp increase in the amount of e-commerce conducted on the Internet. Companies such as Freeserve will receive a percentage of the business conducted on their site. Freeserve's revenue stream will increasingly depend on advertising, sponsorship and online shopping, and eventually this will be greater than the revenues earned from telephone usage. As Freeserve's chief executive explains:

> In three years when people get used to the online business, it will be where they buy their holiday or look for what to do with their kids over the holiday. It will become an everyday tool for them and even if you are only talking about putting a fraction of their spend

through us, I would expect to be able to take a number of pounds off each customer I have got.

The name of the game is gaining customer loyalty and persuading them to part with money. Just how much income Freeserve can generate from each customer is the key to its stock-market valuation. The problem for the free ISPs is that their users tend to be fickle as they have not paid for the service, and may run more than one Internet account.

CHECKLIST

There are many ways to integrate the Web into a marketing strategy, depending on the level of investment available and the level of risk you are prepared to take. Before making a major investment in an Internet project, it is worth considering:

▓ How deep are your pockets, ie how do you plan to finance the 'burn rate'?
▓ Is making profit a priority?
▓ What level of risk are you prepared to take?
▓ Is it important to you to 'get in on the ground floor' and help shape the development of a new medium?

Chapter glossary

ADSL Asymmetrical digital subscriber line, a technology for bringing high-bandwidth information to homes and small businesses over copper telephone lines.

Backbone The cables that carry Internet traffic. Backbones are like highways, except that they carry messages and files. Any message sent on the Internet, whether it's a request to see a Web page or an e-mail, goes first to the ISP, which then sends it into the backbone.

Bandwidth Measures the volume of information that can be passed along a communications link; in digital systems it is measured in bits-per-second (bps). A modem that works at 57,600 bps has twice the bandwidth of a modem working at 28,800 bps. It takes more bandwidth to download large sound files, computer programs and animated videos to acceptable quality than it does photographs or text.

Broadband A telecommunication that provides multiple channels of data over a single communication, for example through fibre-optic cables, which have a 'broad' or unlimited capacity to carry high memory media like video.

Browser The program that enables users to move around the World Wide Web by displaying text and graphics, and creating hypertext connections. See glossary at the end of the book for more details.

Burn rate The rate at which a new company spends its capital while waiting for the operation to become profitable.

Chat Talking to other people who are using the Internet at the same time. These 'real-time' conversations are hosted by chat lines, chat rooms and forums. Participants type in text, which appears on the screen of other participants, who can respond.

Cyberspace A term invented by author William Gibson in *Neuromancer* to describe the place the players of video games imagined behind their screens. It has come to mean where people interact by means of connected computers, eg the Internet. Communication in cyberspace is independent of physical distance.

Data compression A way of reducing the amount of space or bandwidth needed to store or transmit a block of data.

Download Transfer a copy of a file from the Web to your computer.

E-commerce Electronic commerce, or any means of doing business in an automated way.

E-mail Electronic mail. Text messages and computer files exchanged between computers on the Internet.

Extranet A closed network Internet for use between a company and a select group of external organizations.

Fibre-optic cable A new type of cable made from ultra pure glass that uses lasers to transmit data at very high speeds and bandwidths.

Hypertext links Enable Web users to jump from page to page by clicking on underlined text, highlighted images or icons. Also known as hotlinks.

Information superhighway   A term that has come to mean the Internet and its general infrastructure, including private networks, online services, etc.

Internet   An INTERnational NETwork of computers connecting millions of computers all around the world. Services on the Internet include the World Wide Web, e-mail and newsgroups, File Transfer Protocol (FTP), file download facility, and text-based bulletin boards.

Internet Service Provider   Also known as an ISP, Internet access provider or service provider. A business that supplies Internet connection services to individuals, businesses and other organizations.

Intranet   A network designed for information processing within a company or organization. It can be used to distribute documents and software, give access to databases and training, track projects, etc.

MP3 (MPEG Layer 3)   A way of compressing CD-quality music so that it can be downloaded over the Internet. To listen to the files you need an MP3 player such as RealPlayer's RealJukebox, or the latest versions of QuickTime or Microsoft Media Player.

World Wide Web   A service that makes use of the Internet. Based on three programs: Hypertext Transfer Protocol (HTTP) is the standard format that enables computers to connect, exchange information and disconnect quickly. The Uniform Resource Locator (URL or Web address) is a standard method of addressing to enable networking computers to locate each other and make possible the hypertext linking (see above) from one site to another. Hypertext Mark-up Language (HTML) is the language that standardizes the way that Web sites or pages are created.

2

Consumers Online

The World Wide Web can no longer be dismissed as a niche medium for computer experts. The number of people online is growing rapidly, reaching an increasingly wide audience. The shifting demographics are fuelling changes in use. The Web is more than just a world entertainment club only good for aimless 'surfing'; increasingly women, time-pressed middle-aged users, students and senior citizens are looking to the Internet for useful information and the convenience of online services.

HOW MANY ONLINE?

The number of people with access to the Internet and the World Wide Web is growing at a spectacular rate. By September 1999 an estimated 201 million people were using the Internet, representing over 2 per cent of the world population. The numbers, by geographical area, are shown in Table 2.1.

Although the USA has the highest number of Internet users, Finland has more users per capita than any other country. According to a 1998 study by Almanac Inc, over 1.43 million Finnish adults access the Internet, accounting for 37 per cent of the adult population. The second highest number of users per capita is in Norway, with Iceland in third place. The US ranked fourth with 20 per cent of adults online.

There is a bewildering amount of conflicting data and statistics from a variety of sources on Internet and Web usage. This is illustrated by the widely differing 1998 estimates of US users, shown in Table 2.2.

When analysing data on Web penetration, it is important to establish whether or not the sample definition:

▨ relates to all Internet users (people connected to the Internet through an Internet Service Provider enabling them to use

Table 2.1 *Internet users worldwide*

Region	Number of users million	% total
Canada and USA	112	56
Europe	47	23
Asia/Pacific	34	17
Latin America	5	2
Africa	2	1
Middle East	1	<1
Total	201	100

Various sources, compiled by NUA Internet Surveys

Table 2.2 *Comparison of sources*

Millions of Net users 1997–98

Source	Definition	1997	1998
Intertrek	US Total pop	63.0	NA
Intelliquest	US adults 16+	62.0	70.0
Relevant Knowledge	US adults 12+	55.4	57.0
NUA Consultancy	North American adults 18+	54.0	NA
Nielsen Media research	North American adults 18+	52.0	58.0
Morgan Stanley	US adults 18+	50.0	80.0
Find/SVP(CyberDialogue)	US adults 18+	41.5	75.0
Media Matrix	US adults 18+	38.0	NA
Computer Intelligence	US total pop	31.0	NA
MRI	US adults 18+	NA	44.0
eStats	US adults 18+	28.0	47.0

Source: eStats

services such as e-mail and newsgroups) or just those with access to the World Wide Web (for which a browser interface is required in addition to the Internet connection);

■ includes everyone who has ever tried the Internet, those who have used it in the past x months, or regular users;

■ includes 'drop-outs' or people who have tried the Internet but for some reason dropped out.

WHO IS ONLINE?

Quantified and qualitative surveys are now available in many countries to collect the demographic and psychographic profile of Internet users, and limited data on subscribers may be collected by ISPs.

The Web is still male dominated, but women are coming online at a faster rate and now account for around 40 per cent of Internet users in both the US and the UK (according to 1998 reports by eMarketer, Forrester Research and NOP). Women on the Internet range from office workers to stay-at-home 'cybermums'. They have enormous purchasing power and influence: an estimated 70 per cent of women manage household finances, and it is still women who buy the food and household products. This makes the Internet potentially very interesting for marketers targeting women.

Initially there was a lack of compelling content appealing to women but this is changing with the growing number of free sites created specifically for women such as Parent Soup (www.parentsoup.com), iVillage (www.iVillage.com), HomeArts (www.homearts.com) and Women's Wire (www.womenswire. com). The Boots Company and Hollinger Telegraph New Media's joint venture Handbag (www.handbag.com) specifically sets out to target women with 'the best of the world's online services, edited and customized for women in the UK, as well as free Web access, e-mail, expert advice, news, information, interactivity, and online shopping'.

A further factor inhibiting Internet usage by women was their relative lack of technical ability or interest in technology, but as access becomes easier and less dependent on the personal computer (eg, delivered to digital TV through set-top boxes) this inhibition will gradually disappear.

Web usage is extending to the whole family thanks to the increasing availability of personal computers (PCs) outside the work place. Already 41 per cent of children in Britain have access to a PC at home and this will grow as peer pressure plays a significant role in influencing home PC ownership. A 1999 NOP survey shows that over four out of ten British children are now online, and almost half of these have used the Web to browse for something to buy, with 17 per cent having actually made a purchase online. The most popular purchases are games, music, tickets and videos and the most common means of payment is their parents' credit card!

The UK already has the highest usage of the Internet in schools and universities in Europe. The Government target is for all 32,000 British schools to be connected to the World Wide Web by 2002, and millions of pounds are being poured into the development of a National Grid for Learning. The development of screening software (see the list in Useful Contacts and Further Reading) that blocks access to sexually explicit or violent material and to Internet shopping is important: schools have intercepted everything from bomb-making instructions to messages from stalkers on the Internet. The more powerful packages can look at the context as well as the words used, and filter e-mail as well as documents. URLabs' I-Gear package spared teachers the embarrassment of answering questions on the more salacious sections of the Starr Report on President Clinton!

The advent of free service providers (ISPs) has had a dramatic impact not just on the number of Internet users but also the demographic profile. They have attracted a new type of user, generally older and from C2DE social groups, where users previously were predominantly younger and ABC1. A survey carried out by Capibus in 1999 suggests that what UK Internet users have in common is an appetite for new technology. They are more than twice as likely to own a mobile phone as non-users, 72 per cent more likely to have a games console and more than twice as likely to have digital TV.

Broadcasters and political groups around the world use the Internet to deliver their message in increasingly sophisticated ways. A political dissident in China was charged with 'Net subversion' in November 1998, and ethnic Albanian journalists in Kosovo started Radio 21 on the Net. Even the Queen has launched a Royal Web site (www.royal.gov.uk) and the Prince of Wales runs a forum for comments on his Web site (www.princeofwales.gov.uk).

NO LONGER JUST 'COOL' BUT USEFUL

'The folks who used the Internet early on were geeks and hobbyists who didn't have a life off-line,' says Jack Davies, president of AOL International. 'The early adopters are always very different from the mass market. The average person will not spend three hours surfing for cool sites.'

Typically, new Internet users start with e-mail, and then begin to do some general surfing to gain familiarity with the Web. But over time users learn to appreciate the Web's attractions as an information and education medium, and are daily becoming more comfortable and confident about shopping electronically.

A range of useful day-to-day services is now available over the Web, free of charge. Users can follow the latest share prices (and their personal share portfolio) on the *Financial Times'* site (www.FT.com), check the evening's viewing schedule and catch up on events in last night's missed episode of 'EastEnders' on BBC Online (the UK's most visited Web site). They can put in a grocery order to Tesco Direct for home delivery at a pre-arranged time, and do their online banking with National Westminster 24 hours a day. Flight and hotel availability can be checked for business trips, and the family holiday booked.

Usage at work for personal or leisure purposes is decreasing. According to analysts, men are more likely to spend time in aimless 'surfing' than women, who gravitate towards the Web for its sense of community, content and shopping appeals. Working women use the Internet not only to send or respond to e-mail, do business research online and communicate with other employees, but also to bank and shop after retail hours, help with the children's homework, and to work from home. The Internet is perceived to save time, and they value the convenience.

Many Web users have specific destinations in mind when they log on:

▓ Seventy-one per cent of people online seek product information (source: Cyber Dialogue).

▓ The amount of time AOL users spent in chat rooms halved from 40 per cent of total online hours in 1994 to 20 per cent in 1998, while time spent researching prices and purchasing items surged to 23 per cent from almost nothing in 1994.

▓ About 15 per cent of GPs in Britain use the Internet as a source of up-to-date medical and healthcare information (source: NOP).

▓ Just over 40 per cent of junior Internet users in an NOP survey claimed to have visited education sites online and nearly half said they had used the Internet to find information for projects or homework. Almost a quarter had used the Internet to send e-mails or to make friends or communicate with pen pals, a fifth had used the Internet as a dictionary or encyclopaedia and one in ten had used it as a source of information on news and current affairs.

▓ Older users, sometimes referred to as 'silver surfers', are attracted to online financial services.

This new purposefulness even makes the term 'cybersurfer' seem out of date. By the year 2001 it is predicted that the Internet will have become a useful tool in managing everyday activities, with shopping, finance and planning family activities becoming more important than general surfing and typical newsgroup usage.

One of the biggest changes in cyber usage has been in the area of electronic commerce. Despite worries about security, and the belief that shoppers want to touch and feel items before buying them, consumers have shown a willingness to assume some risk in return for the convenience of online shopping. The Internet is the latest time-saving household appliance – women may have money but they no longer have the time to spend it. In a UK survey, just over half of those who had used the Web to purchase a product or service in the past four weeks said they had done so for reasons of 'convenience'.

Although the Internet as a medium transcends national boundaries, local attitudes result in important differences in Internet usage across the key European markets. The prospect of future European monetary and political integration will not necessarily result in a uniformity of usage patterns on the Internet, and organizations seeking to market their products and services via the

Internet across the principal European markets need to tailor their approaches accordingly.

A 1998 European Internet Study conducted by NOP found that as a proportion of the total adult population, the percentage of people who have used the Web in the past four weeks is highest in Britain and Germany (both 9 per cent) and lowest in France (6 per cent).

The relatively low usage in France is largely explained by the existence of Minitel, a proprietary text-based online service provided by France Telecom: many users are unable to see a significant advantage in having access to the Internet over Minitel.

Internet users in Germany are far more likely to use online banking than users in Britain or France, but are far more reserved about disclosing their credit card details over the Internet when making a purchase.

CONSUMER LIFESTYLES

Different consumers have different needs and expectations when they visit the Web. Analysis of the attitudes and motivations of the target market can provide marketers with insight into the type of Web material to which they are most likely to respond.

Forrester Research has developed the Technographics consumer segmentation model to identify those groups of consumers who are most likely to embrace the Internet and other interactive media. They divide US consumers into nine groups defined by income level (low, medium or high) and attitude to technology (optimistic or pessimistic); see Figure 2.1.

Those most likely to use the Internet are the high-income technology optimists. Within this group, the primary motivation for using the Internet differs widely. Some see the Internet and World Wide Web as a convenience, some as an educational tool, some as a source of entertainment. For example:

■ *Fast Forwards* are career-oriented, and have the highest penetration of PCs, the Internet and services that help people manage and make money. They have little spare time and are likely to see home shopping as a time-saving device and be willing to pay a premium for home delivery.

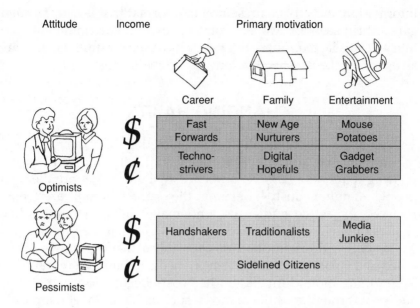

Figure 2.1 *Forrester Technographics segmentation model*
Source: Forrester Research, Inc.

▨ *New Age Nurturers* put their family first, and lead the way in adopting educational software. They may see using the computer as a necessity for their children if they want to get ahead in life. As the family becomes more involved in using interactive tools and the Internet, they spend less time using traditional media.

▨ *Mouse Potatoes* are focused on entertainment, and are quick to adopt satellite and PC-based games. Their primary motivation is interactive entertainment – so they spend a lot less time watching TV and more time interacting with their PC and using the Internet.

While all the above expect an interactive experience on the Web, this may take different forms. For example, busy Fast Forwards demand immediate productivity in the form of an online service or transaction. New Age Nurturers may be less adept with new technology and have slower PCs, and will respond better to detailed information and advice presented in a format that is easy to navigate. Thrill-seeking Mouse Potatoes expect entertainment and interactivity in the form of games, chat and multimedia, and are attracted by the latest technology and gizmos.

CHANGING HABITS

The amount of time people spend interacting with their PCs and the Internet has an impact on their social behaviour and media viewing patterns. Passive audiences where large numbers of people simultaneously consume the same content are being replaced by active audiences who make their own individual choices of what to watch, read and listen to when they want.

This has serious implications for those marketers who have relied in the past on traditional mass media to build their brands. It is becoming more difficult and less cost-effective to reach a mass audience through traditional media such as TV as fewer people are watching and audiences are fragmented across an increasing number of channels. But the potential reach of the Internet is still tiny compared with mass media and the comparative cost per contact varies according to the target market.

UK surveys suggest that time spent online tends to be at the expense of TV viewing: 16–44-year-old Internet users spend an estimated 20 per cent less time watching TV than non-users, and 19 per cent less time listening to the radio. Internet users spend a little more time reading than those who do not use the Internet. In the US, a 1997 Odyssey survey into time substitution showed that 78 per cent of time spent on the Internet was at the expense of TV, 17 per cent came from book-reading time and 11 per cent from magazine reading.

Amongst the younger, computer-literate age groups there is however evidence of 'multi-tasking'. The 1999 NOP survey found that it was common for their sample of children under the age of 17 to listen to music, watch TV, listen to the radio and even read magazines while online. Multiple media campaigns may prove an effective way to reach this group.

Research projects are being established to gain an understanding of the new social dynamics. For example, in the UK the University of Leeds, the Independent Television Commission and Ogilvy and Mather have set up a research project sponsored by business clients to study the impact of technology and the new media on people's behaviour.

A relatively new social phenomenon is the Internet café or *cybercafé*. Coffee and snacks are served as in a normal café, but instead of interacting with each other, customers use the terminals provided to access the Internet. Most cybercafés are small, but one opposite London's Victoria station boasts 400 computer terminals. These are arranged on two floors, divided into sections for experts and beginners. Staff work shifts to provide round-the-clock support for Internet newcomers, and usage costs £1 an hour. Such cafés help to spread the Internet to all-comers at the same time as influencing social habits and behaviour.

The spread of cybercafés may go some way towards countering the claim that the Internet is bad for psychological health and wrecks social life. Interactive enthusiasts claiming that inherently social features like e-mail and Internet chat are more socially healthy than passive mass media, were confounded by the 1998 'Home net' study published in the journal of the American Psychological Association. The survey concluded that the Internet might actually increase the sense of depression and loneliness amongst users. It reported a decline in interaction with family members and a reduced circle of friends directly corresponding to the amount of time participants spent online. This raises questions about the nature of 'virtual communication' and the disembodied relationships formed in cyberspace. Building shallow relationships can lead to an overall decline in feeling of connection to other people – 'like spending all your life at a cocktail party'.

MEETING EXPECTATIONS

The appeal of the Internet to many users is that it puts them in control. Rather than passively receiving media content, they can choose which parts of the Web to visit, in search of information, entertainment, titillation and value-added services. Even if the actual material available differs little from that in other media, the interactivity offered gives the user the illusion of deciding what they want, rather than having it dictated to them. This appeals for example to students and the youth market, who will queue up to use a computer at school, college or home rather than taking a book off the shelf. Parents, advisers and teachers can use this to promote information that might otherwise be dismissed or ignored.

A generation is growing up with access to almost limitless sources of information and channels of communication. They are familiar with computers, the Internet and digital technology and can no longer be expected to be passive recipients of commercial messages. They expect to find customized products and services. They expect not just to read an advertisement but to interact with it for entertainment, to get a service, or to place an order for a product. Successful Web marketing will understand the needs of the 'Net generation', seeking to communicate and provide gratification through an interactive experience.

CHECKLIST

In order to determine whether or not the Web is able to reach your target market, and to understand the needs of your intended audience, various online facilities can be used to supplement traditional research and information sources:

▧   The Internet is a hot news item and gains a lot of coverage in the press. News services and archives such as the FT provide access to international articles with interesting snippets and references to available research. By entering key words to the search facility, you can call up summaries of topics of interest to you, and download reports (some free of charge, some for a small fee).

▧   A number of research company Web sites offer free data. For example, up-to-date international statistics on Internet usage, surveys and related topics are provided on the NUA Web pages (www.nua.ie/how-many-online and www.nua.ie/surveys). Summaries of recent research surveys in Europe and particularly the UK are provided by the NOP Research Group on www.nopres.co.uk/surveys. These sites offer not only free statistics but also links to other relevant sources on the Web.

For details of other paid-for Internet research companies, see Useful Contacts and Further Reading.

Chapter glossary

Cybercafé   A coffee shop or restaurant that offers access to PCs or other terminals that are connected to the Internet, usually for a per-hour or per-minute fee. Users are encouraged to buy food and drink while accessing the Internet.

Geek   Originally a circus term for a performer who bit off chickens' heads, adopted to refer to those Internet users who spout technical jargon, acronyms and computer codes.

3

Market Review

New competitors and business models are emerging with the help of Web technology and the increasing acceptance of electronic commerce. Entrepreneurial start-up businesses offer convenience and imaginative new services. As new competitors and business models emerge, traditional businesses may need to respond by reviewing the way they do business.

EVOLUTION OR REVOLUTION?

In some markets the Internet may just represent an extension of existing business opportunities. It can be an additional means of communicating to a closely targeted market, or have potential as a new distribution channel to complement traditional delivery systems. However, it is dangerous to make the assumption that the new technology will have no real impact on the business without taking a closer look. It opens the door to competitors with revolutionary ideas on how to redefine the business model, and in some industries this is already radically influencing the whole way of doing business.

Electronic commerce (e-commerce)

This is more than just electronic retailing (or *e-tailing* as it is sometimes called). E-commerce uses electronic means to facilitate a full range of business operations, from helping to generate demand, to fulfilling orders, managing payments and providing ongoing support facilities. It can cut expenses by reducing transaction costs, and be used to streamline business processes such as supply chain management.

E-commerce is not a new phenomenon in the business-to-business context: big companies have been using Electronic Data Interchange (EDI) for years to simplify the way they source their supplies. But as the Internet grows, selling to private individuals over the Web is becoming widespread. Manufacturers and service suppliers are in direct contact with buyers, eliminating the need for a middleman or agent.

'Disintermediation'

Bypassing the middleman may result in lower costs. Web entrepreneurs can reduce prices and draw buyers away from traditional agents and established high-street businesses. This has had a significant impact in some areas. For example, the Dell Computer Corporation makes computers and sells them direct to the consumer: it doesn't sell through retailers, as it doesn't need them. In the travel sector, a growing percentage of online airline tickets will be bought directly from the airlines rather than through online travel agents. Traditional retailers of books and CDs have been hit by online retailers, and real estate in the US is increasingly traded on the Web.

In response to the threat of *disintermediation*, some traditional middlemen (or intermediaries) are adapting their business models to take advantage of the Web. If you are going to be cannibalized by a new business model, it might as well be one of your own offshoots.

Charles Schwab
www.schwab.com

Online investing is now the second most popular pursuit on the Internet after sex. Investors can get quotes and research, place orders at any hour of the day or night, and transfer funds in and out of their accounts without ever having to speak to a broker or pay their hefty fees. This do-it-yourself model of investing has its dangers as online traders are unsupervised and often unskilled, and investment information gleaned from the Internet is often unreliable. But people like the sense of empowerment they get from the Net when deciding whether to buy or sell, and Forrester Research estimates that 3.1 million American families will be investing online by the end of 1999, and 9.7 million by 2003.

When US broker Charles Schwab entered the world of online broking, it predicted that doing so could cost as much as US $120 million (£75 million) in lost commission from trades that would previously have gone through conventional channels attracting higher fees. By going online, Schwab was to an extent cannibalizing its own business. But online trading has proved such a success that in June 1999 Schwab's market capitalization exceeded that of rival Merrill Lynch. Charles Schwab Europe was launched in April 1998, and a year later was Britain's largest online broker with customers joining at a rate of 500 to 1000 each week.

In response to competition from online trading, Merrill Lynch has now come to the dramatic decision to allow its customers to trade shares online and pay lower commission. This new hybrid model of trading both online and offline, dubbed 'clicks and mortar' by Schwab, is seen as the future of world share trading.

'Infomediaries'

A new generation of middlemen is now appearing that will shift power from sellers to buyers. *Infomediaries* are agents who sift and repackage the wealth of data available on the Web, aggregating and syndicating electronic content collected from dozens of sources to create special interest reports for businesses and individuals.

In the past, companies and agents have often been able to control the flow of information available to customers and so control the market. But with the information provided by infomediaries, businesses and individuals can compare products and search for the best deal. For example, electronic shopping agents compare prices and products to get the best deal for buyers (see Chapter 9). Europe's first Internet-based cooperative buying company Letsbuyit (www.letsbuyit.co.uk) allows shoppers to pool their purchasing power and get discounts from manufacturers on goods ranging from televisions to sports bags.

The flow of information provided by infomediaries ultimately creates markets controlled by consumers for consumers, buyers' market. It applies constant downward pressure on sellers' profit margins, because everyone will instantly know what everyone else is charging for any particular standard product. Buying power can be aggregated without revealing the details of the individuals represented, and this undermines attempts by direct marketing to establish a one-to-one relationship with their consumers.

Increased competition
The Web may also redefine the market and competitors. New competitors will be attracted by the reduced costs of doing business and the limited barriers to entry. The Web transcends regional and national boundaries, and offers 24-hour access to a global marketplace. Companies can access new markets without establishing a physical presence locally, and speak directly to consumers and service their needs through electronic means. For example, ING Direct can run a successful bank in Canada without investing millions of dollars in building a branch network across the country. For the Yorkshire-based English Teddy Bear company, the Web has opened up new opportunities. 'Seventy-five percent of the customers who visit our shops are already from overseas,' says the managing director. 'But we have just had a £7,000 order via the Internet from Malaysia. No customer is going to come through our doors and buy £7,000 worth of teddy bears to take back overseas.'

Trading via the Web opens up both opportunities and threats, particularly where big pricing differentials exist between markets. Foreign competitors now have direct access to consumers in 'rip-off Britain' and can offer cheaper prices on a range of merchandise.

The Web is no respecter of size and tradition, and small and entrepreneurial start-up businesses with innovative propositions can take advantage of the Web. New entrants and start-up businesses may be attracted by the opportunity to capitalize on the relatively low cost of setting up a 'virtual store'. The cost of setting up a prime site on the high street has long been a barrier to entry for small businesses. But it is no longer crucial to have a high-street presence or a physical office in order to access potential customers.

For example, London-based wine merchant Bibendum has decided to expand its operation by shutting its conventional shop in Primrose Hill, London. The company has a turnover of about £20 million servicing the hotel, restaurant, supermarket, off-licence and private business sectors. When the business was founded in 1982, all of its clients visited its Primrose Hill retail outlet, but over time business has gradually transferred to the phone, fax and e-mail. With the growth of the Internet, Bibendum management has taken the plunge and decided to commit to an electronic commerce system linking online ordering to stock control and billing systems (www.bibendum-wine.co.uk). Sales and marketing are conducted through the Web site, while the high-street shop is now used for regular wine-tasting sessions for clients.

Virtual stores can be almost infinite in size. Amazon can offer more books than any physical bookshop could stock, and can also have a music offering as large as that of any other online music store. In fact Amazon only carries stock of the 1,000 top-selling books itself, and relies on the physical proximity of its offices to the largest wholesaler of books, Ingram Book Company, which stocks 40,000 titles and provides 59 per cent of Amazon sales. But with a sophisticated search tool and an index page, Amazon offers a complete bookshop and a complete music shop under one name.

Reduced barriers to entry and the rapid growth in Internet usage will encourage a greater number of suppliers to enter the market. This, in conjunction with improved information and 'empowered' customers, is likely to put downward pressure on prices and create a potential new competitive threat. Existing institutions may find they need to reinforce their business with value-added services. For example, the rapid growth of book sales over the Web has caused high-street bookstores to re-examine what they can offer their customers in terms of added value. It is no longer enough to compete on price and convenience, and the range of titles that a high-street bookshop can hold in stock cannot compete with an Internet bookshop. This has forced traditional bookshops to respond by providing reading seats, in-store coffee shops and customer service desks in an attempt to create the sort of atmosphere in which customers are happy to browse.

THE RACE FOR CRITICAL MASS

In order to generate a stream of revenue from advertising and sales on the Web it is crucial to attract a significant audience. Just as out-of-town shopping centres influence the purchasing patterns of large numbers of shoppers, so sites that control Web traffic stand to gain huge strategic advantages. Companies are manoeuvring to become the major ports of entry to the Web, known as *'portals'*.

For the average visitor the vast Web has become confusing, with its millions of different sites to visit, range of search facilities, multitude of information sources and constantly changing services. Portals recognize the power they can wield by providing users with a structure and sense of organization, and typically offer search facilities, content, links to the best sites and e-mail services. They aim to build brand loyalty and encourage visitors to spend more time with them. The longer people stay, the more advertisements site owners can display and the bigger the revenue they can rake in from merchants who want to link with the site.

ISPs and browsers are obvious contenders for portal status as they are the starting points for millions of visitors using the Web. They have the advantage that they provide the services that get people on to the Internet, rather than simply offering a service to those already online. They can turn their *home pages* – the place most visitors first arrive at – into personalized electronic pages where visitors can check share prices, sports scores, the weather and news headlines, read messages, drop in at chat rooms and play games. By bringing together information from multiple sources they provide 'one-stop surfing', cutting down on virtual travelling from site to site, and provide direct links to shopping and advice services. The attraction for retailers such as Tesco and Dixons in offering Internet access is controlling their user base and generating loyalty through the service provided.

Search engines, media and community sites and telecommunications companies are putting together deals and partnerships in the race to achieve a significant volume of traffic. Most channel their viewers towards outside Internet retailers under sponsorship deals, but in an effort to distinguish itself from its rivals, search engine Lycos announced its intention of going into business as a retailer, setting up its own Internet department store.

Search engines initially sent visitors on to other Web sites immediately, on the grounds that the faster they pointed people to other
sites, the better they were doing. Then they realized the potential
of keeping Web surfers as long as possible. Their strategy now is to
provide reasons to stay in, or 'stickiness'. Games are the latest addition to the range of services offered by portals: their attraction is
that they tend to keep users on a site for a long period, during
which time they can be presented with advertisements.

Advertisers are likely to be drawn by the prospect of a 'mass-
market' finally taking shape if they are able to reach their audience
by placing advertisements on portals. However, there is no guarantee that the millions of visitors using a portal site either see or
respond to advertisements placed there. The question of advertising efficacy remains key.

The value of these portals lies in the strength of their brand
names, and their ability to sell advertising space and offer online
shopping services. Microsoft, Netscape, America Online, Yahoo!,
Excite and Compaq have spent millions of dollars transforming
their Web sites into starting points for Internet surfing and establishing strong brand recognition. But there are hundreds of companies vying for position as portals and they cannot all succeed. The
online advertising market is still small and unlikely to be able to
support more than a handful of key portals. Even with the
dramatic rise in e-commerce activity, many predict that a shake out
is on the horizon.

THE 'FIRST MOVER' ADVANTAGE

There is a widely held belief that in a few years, a handful of
players will dominate in any one sector online. First-comers will be
in a prime position to capitalize on profit opportunities as the Web
matures: they argue that those that lag behind may have to be
content with niche positions. This is the thinking behind the rush
to throw money into the race for market share. 'This is a land grab,'
declared the CEO of iVillage to *Fortune* magazine in 1998. 'You
want to put your stakes in the most valuable property you can as
fast as you can because it's not going to be there tomorrow.'

Amazon and most other online retailers have been prepared to
spend vast sums of money on marketing and go on losing money.

In fact Amazon has announced that it doesn't expect to make money for some time. But once an online retailer has invested the considerable sums necessary to establish a brand and to attract customers, it can crush the competition and extend the range of offerings. Presumably the long-term hope is that having gained a dominant market position, it can start to charge higher prices.

Amazon – part 1
www.amazon.com

Amazon pioneered the development of the fast-growing online book market and has succeeded in building one of the best-known Internet brands from scratch in just a few years. With a combination of aggressive pricing, a powerful search facility, extensive customer information and book reviews to aid selection, Amazon has achieved high growth. Its revenue of US $16 million in 1996, representing 3 per cent of e-commerce in that year, grew to more than US $100 million in 1997, during which it went public, gaining US $50 million funding.

Amazon's estimated marketing and advertising costs came to US $26 per sale in 1998, compared with US $2.50 for traditional bookstores. Amazon has yet to make a profit, yet its shares soared and the company was valued at US $17 billion at the end of 1998, double the combined value of Barnes and Noble, and Borders, America's two largest bookstore chains.

Amazon attracted more than 3 million customers in 1998 and sold US $203 million worth of books. When Barnes and Noble (which possesses a strong offline brand name and has the opportunity to advertise the online store in its regular bookshops) entered the market with huge marketing investment, it generated only US $22 million in revenue in the first half of 1998 and attracted only 700,000 customers.

The Amazon brand has been expanded beyond books to include CDs and videos, a drugstore and online auctions. It has announced its intention to launch toys and consumer electronics, software, home improvements, video games and gifts. Amazon is not really a bookstore at all. It can be viewed as a customer base to which the company will sell all kinds of goods, using the same easy instant-ordering interface. And when that happens, conventional companies will start to feel the heat in the same way that traditional book giants such as Barnes and Noble have been hit by Amazon's success in the book field.

COMPETITIVE RESPONSE

As already discussed, the costs of entry for new competitors on the Web are very low. And as the technology behind infomediaries and shopping agents develops, consumers will be able to find the lowest price. This will restrict the ability of established online retailers to put their prices up on standardized products to the level at which they can turn in a profit.

Amazon – part 2

The growing number of local rivals has forced Amazon to launch in the UK (www.amazon.co.uk) and Germany (www.amazon.de) in order to remain competitive on price and delivery timings.

In the UK a price war broke out when established high-street book retailer WH Smith launched its own online book service offering huge discounts. As a result, in summer 1999 WH Smith Online were selling best-selling hardbacks for 60 per cent less than the jacket price.

WH Smith has an established brand name and 'deep pockets', as the parent business is profitable. But how long can Amazon continue to invest and not make a profit? It remains to be seen whether Amazon's first mover advantage is sufficiently strong to fight off such competition. In an environment where consumers hold the balance of power, how loyal will they prove to pioneer Amazon?

When asked during the 1999 Industry Standard Internet Summit whether he was concerned about developments leading to an environment of perfect information, Amazon founder Jeff Bezos replied that he worried to the same extent as Boeing worries about gravity!

Some established businesses are taking Web initiatives now as pre-emptive or defensive action even where the investment of resources delivers no obvious financial return in the short term. For example, it is unlikely that Tesco's Home Shopping service is profitable (the £5 delivery charge does not cover additional logistics costs incurred), but the company is both gaining early experience of e-commerce and pre-empting the entry of purely

Web-based 'virtual grocers' as seen in the US (www.peapod.com, www.netgrocer.com).

Other companies are adopting a strategy of wait and see... let the first movers pioneer the way, invest large sums of money and build the market. Some will be successful in creating powerful new brands from scratch, and some may even make money too. Others, like the much trumpeted but ill-fated push channel PointCast, will be quietly sold off at a loss to their original investors. Lessons will be learnt, and many companies will prefer to watch this happen before leaping in.

CHECKLIST

Every business needs to review the market and decide what implications competitor activities are likely to have. It is important to think laterally in order to explore the opportunities afforded by the Internet... and to anticipate how Web entrepreneurs may turn the existing business model on its head:

■ Conduct an audit of competitor Web activity. This can be done by visiting competitor Web sites: if you do not know the URL or Web address, type in the name of the brand or company on one of the search engines and a list of matches will be created. The search engines all work slightly differently and people have their personal favourites. Yahoo! is one of the most commonly used, and you can search under different categories such as 'business and economy', 'news and media', 'entertainment' and so on. This can be a time-consuming exercise, and one that can be delegated either internally or to external consultants.

■ Consider drawing up a good old-fashioned SWOT analysis to identify how your business' strengths and weaknesses stack up against the industry opportunities and competitor threats.

■ Look at markets other than your own in order to get fresh ideas. It may be possible to transfer the business model from a completely unrelated market to transform your own.

■ Subscribe to a news service to keep abreast of market activities. For example, FT.com offers a free 'news by e-mail' service where you can specify the topics you want to hear about, such as 'Internet and e-commerce'.

Chapter glossary

Disintermediation   Cutting out the middleman.

E-tailing   Electronic retailing.

Home page   The opening screen of a Web site that welcomes and guides the visitor to the facilities available.

Infomediary   An agent that uses information technology to gather, analyse and redistribute information.

Portal   The point of entry to the Web. Also known as gateways, portals are typically ISPs and browsers who set their Web site as the default opening page for visitors, and search engines. The major portals are extending the services they offer in an attempt to encourage visitors to stay on their site as long as possible, and so attract advertising revenue.

Search engine   A service that indexes, organizes and often reviews Web sites. Users can search for information by entering key words. Different types of search engine work in different ways. Major search engines include Excite, Infoseek, Lycos and Yahoo!

Stickiness   The qualities that induce visitors to remain at a Web site rather than move on to another site. Portals achieve stickiness first of all by having a great deal of content, but also by finding ways to involve the user with the site.

4

User Benefits

Don't expect users to beat a path to your door simply because you have a Web site. There are millions of possible destinations for Web surfers, so a product or service must offer something that users want, and in a way that exploits the interactive capabilities of the Web.

AN INTERACTIVE EXPERIENCE

There are millions of Web destinations competing for attention, and Web surfers are increasingly sophisticated and demanding in what they expect to gain from their visit. A Web site must offer its target customers a 'reason why' to attract them, and the benefit should be something that the user wants, delivered in a way that other media or channels cannot. There is no advantage to be had from seeing exactly the same advertisement, product information or service as is available through other media and channels.

The main attribute distinguishing the Web from traditional mass media is *interactivity*. While TV and radio broadcast one-way messages (monologue) and provide a passive experience, the Web opens up new possibilities for identifying and satisfying user needs. But there is more to interactivity than impressing the visitor with clever animation and audio tricks. True interactivity engages the visitor in two-way communication: a dialogue.

The most widely used interactive facility on the Internet is e-mail. Businesses and individuals alike have readily adopted this quick and efficient means of conducting a dialogue. Other examples of common interactive uses of the Web are:

■ information services;
■ online transaction facilities;
■ customer services;
■ advice and problem solving;
■ online communities and chat rooms;
■ games;
■ surveys.

The most appropriate use of interactivity will depend on the type of product or service to be marketed.

THE BENEFIT

Some products are more naturally suited to online promotion and sales than others. Commercial exploitation of the Web has been led by high interest products and services that consumers are likely to seek out actively on the Web. The main benefits a product or service can offer on the World Wide Web are information, customization, convenience and confidentiality.

Information

Products and services that are information-intensive tend to adapt well to the Web. The Internet is technically very good for handling information, as it offers:

■ access to a wealth of data: unlimited storage capacity in cyber-space;
■ personalization: processing in response to individual specifications;
■ speed and 24-hour availability: up-to-date data at the click of a mouse.

In a society where information has a high value, the Web presents a cheap method of distribution. The Internet has become a key tool for *'knowledge management'* within companies, and for the exchange of data between businesses.

Products benefiting from effective distribution of information are as diverse as academic institutions offering details of courses and online application facilities, data-rich services such as the financial and consultancy sectors, banking services and newspaper archive services.

For example, National Westminster Bank (www.natwest.co.uk) is rolling out its online banking service to small businesses and individual customers. The NatWest On-Line service promises a simple, convenient and secure way to bank 24 hours a day, pay bills at the touch of a button and check all account details instantly. Any standard PC can be used, and the service is supported by a free 24-hour customer helpdesk. Payments and transfers can be scheduled in advance for automatic payment, money transferred between NatWest accounts, and account information downloaded into a range of financial management packages.

Many people are prepared to spend hours researching information on high interest, high value products such as cars and property. Information sites can be used to bring buyers and sellers together.

For example, BMW has set up a popular site that offers its Approved Used Car Database (www.bmw.co.uk). BMW's dealers contribute to up-to-date listings of all the used cars on their lots, and visitors can search by model, colour, series or region, and get directions to all 160 dealerships. BMW UK estimates that in 1998 up to 40 per cent of its new leads in the UK were generated by the site.

Sites can also link through to finance and insurance sites. The Web is particularly good at allowing buyers to search for cars by specification rather than just the make or model. Some people may have particular requirements like air-conditioning and a CD player, and sophisticated Web sites allow this kind of search.

Customization

The combination of data storage capacity, speed (which facilitates interactivity) and personalization helps to make customization a viable alternative to mass marketing in some markets. Companies traditionally minimize costs by maintaining a core product and attempting to reach multiple market segments by manipulating elements of the mix. But interactivity can define the needs of small market segments and individual customers, allowing products and services to be adapted and tailored accordingly. Customers can be invited to define the specifications of a product or package which is then built to order, and services can be personalized according to the needs of the individual.

Dell
www.dell.com, www.euro.dell.com

Customers can choose from hundreds of configurations when they order a computer from Dell Computer Corporation. Dell started by selling personal computers through the computer press, using mail and the telephone to undercut dramatically its rivals. Its experience in telephone sales gave it a natural head start when it came to understanding how the Web could be exploited. Dell now sells more than US $40 million worth of personal computers and peripherals online a day to individuals and businesses.

The Web site provides all the services that are available by telephone, plus a configuration service that helps users to tailor the computer they want and to calculate the price (see Figure 4.1). Configuring a computer is the kind of task that can be done effectively by electronic means, as it is well specified but highly complex and so prone to human error.

The site acts as catalogue, sales clerk, after-sales assistant, complaints department, technical manual and repair technician rolled into one, providing a customized route for each customer. Having configured their desired computer system, customers can place an order and track its progress from manufacture in Ireland to shipping. Once they receive the PC, customers can get online support and download software upgrades.

The influence of the Web site cannot be measured simply through online sales, as many visitors still place their orders by fax or telephone:

> We don't see Dell.com as a competing channel. We see it as a complementary channel. A lot of people visit Dell.com and then call us on the telephone and buy. Is that a bad thing? No, because it takes six to eight telephone calls to sell a computer, and we just made five of them go away, with a commensurate reduction in operating

expenses. (Hill, K, 1997, Electronic marketing: The Dell computer experience, in *Electronic Marketing and the Consumer*, ed R A Peterson, Sage, London. Taken from *Marketing Business*, June 1999.)

Figure 4.1 *DIY computers with Dell*

Convenience

The Web can save people time and effort. Time-pressed groups such as Forrester's 'Fast Forwards' (see Chapter 2) appreciate the convenience of being able to conduct both business and personal transactions in their own time from the comfort of their home or from the office. Business deals, personal banking and the regular grocery order can be done with minimum fuss, leaving more time for leisure activities.

For example, organizing a wedding can be a lot of hassle. Finding a venue, buying outfits, setting up a wedding present list, arranging the cake, the cars and the flowers, choosing readings and hymns for a church ceremony... Web Weddings (www.webwedding.co.uk) is a start-up venture that draws together companies and services needed by couples in planning a wedding, providing a convenient one-stop shopping directory. The information is broken down by region so it is easy for brides and grooms to find and book everything. It aims to finance itself through advertising revenue from the thousands of wedding-oriented businesses that can advertise on the site and by taking a percentage of sales through their sites. It also offers free Web pages for couples to post details ahead of their wedding, a chat area for brides to swap ideas and hints, and plans to include celebrity input.

When it comes to home shopping, the convenience factor tends to outweigh any need to see, touch or feel the items in categories where products are assumed to be of consistent quality. Some of the greatest early successes (in turnover terms) on the Web have been in online sales of books and CDs. Books and CDs from a reputable source are assumed to be consistent in quality and do not need to be inspected individually. In the same way, consumers are more likely to appreciate the convenience of home delivery for products such as dry groceries that do not need to be seen or touched before a purchase is made, than fresh fruit and vegetables.

After-sales customer support and order tracking can be provided through e-mail links from a Web site to the customer services department. A Frequently Asked Questions (FAQ) page answering such questions and giving trouble-shooting tips is useful, and some products (such as software companies, information services) can supply fixes and updates electronically. All these add to the ease and convenience of making a transaction on the Web.

Confidentiality/anonymity

Sex and pornography are best sellers on the Web. The top ten terms that were reportedly entered on to search engine Alta Vista in 1997 say it all:

1. sex;
2. nude;
3. pictures;
4. jpg (J-PEG is a format for online photos);
5. software;

6. windows;
7. adult;
8. women;
9. naked;
10. erotic.

The Internet is useful for products that do not need face-to-face interaction with the seller, particularly where there is an embarrassment factor or where anonymity is an advantage, for example condoms and sex aids. People appreciate the apparent anonymity and confidentiality afforded by an electronic transaction (not always realizing that once material is downloaded from the Web, a record is kept on the computer's hard disk!).

A product does not need to be pornographic to benefit from some discretion. The Web enables products of an emotional or personal nature to target one or many distinct audience groups, and to speak to consumers individually and in confidence. This allows for longer, more intimate interactions and deeper information than, for example, do broadcast media. The brand is accessible 24 hours a day, seven days a week, opening the door for an intimate dialogue.

For example, Procter & Gamble (P&G) has developed a series of Web sites targeting particular groups of consumers from teenagers to pensioners, in line with their stated intention to shift marketing spend from mass media. The lion's share of P&G's online marketing budget is behind brands such as Always panty liners, Tampax tampons, Pampers nappies, Cover Girl makeup and Olean fat substitute. These are all personal or intimate products.

The Tampax site (www.tampax.com) provides a discussion forum for women's issues, and the Pampers Web site (www.pampers.com) has been turned into the 'Pampers Parenting Institute', addressing various issues of concern to new or expectant mothers. 'Our site lets a woman who is pregnant explore what will happen to her in private, so she doesn't have to ask stupid questions. That's as emotional as you can get in that context.'

LOW-INVOLVEMENT PRODUCTS

Products and services that have adapted easily to the Web tend to be those where consumers feel highly involved in the purchase decision, because they are areas of high interest and/or high value. Many people are happy to spend time seeking out information on the latest model of car, and research ways in which to cut down the cost of going on holiday or buying a house.

But for many product categories, conducting e-commerce over the Web does not seem so practical. Many everyday, low-value products such as household cleaners and packaged groceries are of relatively little consumer interest, while items such as confectionery and soft drinks are often impulse purchases. For such low-involvement, mass-produced goods:

▓ Most information needs can be satisfied through the interactivity of a free telephone number.
▓ Customization or building to order is impractical, as extending an already comprehensive range of variants only adds to supply chain costs.
▓ The logistics of online sales and the cost of physical distribution to individual addresses of low-value, bulky products may not be commercially viable.
▓ Setting up direct sales to consumers runs the risk of antagonizing traditional retailers on whom the brand depends for general distribution.

Yet even everyday low-involvement products can find ways to exploit the interactive online environment. Leading brand manufacturers such as Procter & Gamble, Unilever and many others are committed to finding ways to use the Internet to promote their packaged goods.

While in high-interest categories the pull of the product or service alone is enough, the challenge for everyday, low-interest products is how to attract customers to their Web site. They cannot rely on basic product information to be of sufficient interest to pull in many visitors, but can develop a service that adds value to their offering.

ADDING VALUE

Low-interest products need to give something of value to the consumer in exchange for listening to their marketing message. The Web can be used not just to sell to consumers but also to create a value-added proprietary service offering benefits such as utility, education, entertainment and a sense of community.

Utility

Practical online services may be designed to help busy consumers access useful information and expert advice on related topics. Personalized communications allow the relevance of the brand message to be maximized according to the profile and needs of an individual.

'Meal solution' sites are common, as the provision of ideas and recipes meets a recurring need amongst the target group of housewives. There are numerous examples of sites offering recipe services and meal solutions (typically from food companies and grocery retailers). Tips from the 'category expert' give advice and information, such as Persil's 'SOS stains' line (www.persil.co.uk), which answers questions about how to remove different types of stains from clothing.

Education

Brands with credibility are able to attract visitors seeking more knowledge of the industry and related issues. Education services may be directly related to the product category, or on a subject that is particularly appropriate to the target market.

For example, Nestlé's Willy Wonka Candy Factory (www.wonka.com) has a basic tutorial on Web technology, and a technology trivia quiz for kids, which helps to gain the acceptance of parents and teachers.

Cadbury
www.cadbury.co.uk, www.cadbury.au, www.yowie.co.uk,
www.cadburylearningzone.co.uk

Cadbury has always adopted a market-leading role in the UK and in its major markets around the world. It provides considerable amounts of information about the origins of chocolate and chocolate confectionery, its brands and current events in its marketing programme. 'Cadbury World' in Birmingham allows the public to explore the history of chocolate, the cultural heritage of the company and to visit parts of the factory in operation. In particular Cadbury provides educational material for schools as part of curriculum material for industry-based projects.

The advent of the Internet has enabled much of the information to be made available via the Web. The Australian-based Cadbury's Yowie Web site (www.cadbury.au) provides teachers with a full downloadable pack of lesson plans, homework and activity sheets for a Yowie Ecology Project. Yowie was introduced into the UK in 1999, and the UK version of the site introduces the Yowie characters and gives a virtual guide to their native habitat (woodlands, wetlands, waterways, etc; see Figure 4.2). Visitors can wander around and click on different areas to learn about the environment and ecological issues.

Figure 4.2 *Explore the Yowies' natural environment*

The Cadbury Marketing Manager explains:

> The Yowie concept is an integrated marketing proposition, with a series of chocolate characters, collectable animal figures and many other associated products, books and soft toys. The role played by the Web site is to animate the Yowie environment, and to provide a platform for collectors and participants to become involved with these entrancing little characters.

Cadbury also plans to launch a Yowie educational site in 2000, under the Cadbury Learning Zone on the Web (www. cadburylearningzone.co.uk). This will support the National Curriculum and provide information for teachers and pupils in the areas of environmental studies and geography.

But not every brand can set itself up as a category expert. Consumers are often sophisticated, advertising literate and cynical about the motivations of brand-inspired offers, and professionals are likely to turn to the extensive non-commercial resources available and independent consumer experts for objective information.

Entertainment

Image and fun-related product categories commonly adopt this route, particularly where the target audience is young and technologically literate.

Soft drinks, snacks and confectionery, where the information route is not very appropriate, offer games and music – see Tango (www.tango.co.uk), Irn-bru (www.irn-bru.co.uk), Pepsi-Cola (www.pepsi.com and www.pepsi.co.uk) and Pringles (www. pringles.com).

Some car manufacturers keen to exploit the cult status of their models among a new generation of potential buyers, such as the Mini and the Volkswagen Beetle, use entertainment to add interest. The Mini site (www.mini.co.uk) invites visitors to enter brand-related competitions (eg design their own Mini) and games such as 'sardines' (how many people can you fit into a Mini?) and offers screensavers to download. Visitors to the New Beetle Web site (www.newbeetle.co.uk) can drive a virtual Beetle and earn points by flashing the lights or sounding the horn in response to oncoming vehicles, losing points if they flash police cars.

Uploaded (www.uploaded.com), the online version of laddish magazine *Loaded*, and *FHM* (www.fhm.co.uk) provide entertainment rather than information on their online magazines. Content is updated daily, with such features as joke of the day and position of the week.

A sense of community

Creating a community of interest encourages people to keep returning to a Web site. *Chat rooms, bulletin boards* and competitions encourage visitors to participate and to interact with other like-minded people.

The Football Association site sponsored by Carling Black Label (www.fa-premier.com) has created discussion groups for each football club. People register on entrance into their club's discussion groups, and then go on to discuss (in endless and meticulous detail) the ins and outs of their beloved team.

Mum
www.mum-online.co.uk

There are few people who would actively seek out an anti-perspirant deodorant Web site out of interest in the product alone. The Mum marketing team knew when it set out to build a Web site that it had to offer more than just brand information to attract its target audience of women.

Mum-online aims to create a virtual community for women, to help women find their way through 'the tangled World Wide Web to the best information'. *Hotlinks* are provided to about 500 hand-picked sites of relevance to women in the UK. As the Mum agency account director explained in *E-volve* (May 1999):

> It was important that the sites were carefully researched because there are so many bad ones out there. Also, many that you come across and think are good are actually based in the US, which could lead to delivery charges for customers.

The selected sites are divided into key areas of interest, as shown in Figure 4.3.

Figure 4.3 *Mum's choice*

The Mum site also includes:

▥ a bulletin board where consumers can post questions on any
  subject, from the menopause through savings accounts to stain
  removal. They then wait for responses from other users;
▥ a quarterly free prize draw: participants are e-mailed to tell
  them if they have won or not, and invited to revisit the site to
  enter the next draw;
▥ a history of the Mum brand;
▥ recommendations on which Mum fragrance to choose.

Adding value in the form of practical information, education and
entertainment services may successfully attract the attention of
consumers and offer a tangible benefit. But the cost of maintaining
these services is often difficult to justify commercially unless they
can be shown to stimulate sales. Companies that started out using
the Web as a new vehicle for building brand image are increasingly
looking for ways to convert goodwill into hard sales.

Boots the Chemist
www.boots.co.uk

Boots the Chemist enjoys a unique position in British life as a trusted expert in family health and beauty, with a reputation as an ethical and socially responsible company.

The Boots Web site was first set up in 1996 with the objective of adding value to the consumer in the form of free information and entertainment. It also offered useful services such as the latest weather report for European cities in the sun care section and teenage chat forums. There was little mention of brands and products, and no 'hard sell'.

Based on what was learnt from this early Web site, Boots relaunched the Web site in 1999 as an integral part of its marketing strategy. The Boots management team came to the conclusion that free information and entertainment alone are not sustainable as a business model:

> Research showed that the Web site should be based on three corner-stones: content, community and commerce. In terms of content, consumers want fast moving and personalized information, and this is what will bring them back to the site again and generate loyalty and repeat business. A sense of community not only encourages people to share their thoughts and issues with other like-minded people, but also provides interesting content for the site. But commerce is key in the long term for the revenue stream.

Commerce, or the commercial impact of the site, means not just online sales, but also any activities influencing customer choice leading to purchases in-store. The relaunched site, shown in Figure 4.4, aims to replicate and enhance what consumers find in-store, with help and advice but no obligation to buy, and online experts and celebrities to add authority. A condensed range of some 3,000 products is available for sale online (less than 10 per cent of the full store range but offering something from each category). This is seen as a complementary service rather than source of cannibalization, offering customers a choice of shopping means to suit different moods and needs. Some revenue will be earned from brand sponsorship and advertising, but Boots will always take responsibility for content and make the distinction between brand-sponsored messages and independent advice quite clear.

Figure 4.4 *Boots relaunch*

CHECKLIST

Put yourself in the shoes of the consumer or end user, and consider:

▓ the key benefit on offer;
▓ how this can be presented interactively, in a manner that is different from other media and other competing products;
▓ how interactivity adds value to the proposition.

Chapter glossary

Bulletin board A host computer that is accessible by dial-up phone. Many bulletin board systems have Web sites, and many ISPs have bulletin board systems from which Internet users can download the software needed to get connected. Bulletin boards often offer chat and images for downloading.

Chat room Where users can participate in a discussion by typing their contribution in on the keyboard. This is displayed within seconds on screen, and other users can respond. Some chat rooms are screened for inappropriate material, but many are left unsupervised, leading to some steamy and explicit contributions!

Hotlink A hyperlink that enables users to jump between Web pages or sites by clicking on underlined text, highlighted images or icons.

Interactivity A two-way communication in which the Web user can participate. An active rather than passive experience.

Knowledge management A fashionable new term to describe the concept of deciding what information should and can be shared within an organization, and using technology to distribute that information. This often involves an intranet.

5

Strategy and Responsibilities

It is all too easy to get carried away with enthusiasm for the new medium with its exciting technology surrounded by hype and jargon. The reasons for investing in the Web need to be closely scrutinized, and activities should be an integral part of the brand or company strategy. Synergies with other media can be found only if the objectives and communication message are consistent. It is the role of marketing to set brand objectives, work with the IT department to find solutions and ensure that adequate resources are made available.

COMMERCIAL OBJECTIVES

In the excitement of jumping on the Web bandwagon, many companies have followed the crowd and, in knee-jerk fashion, built a Web site because it seemed like a cool thing to do, or because the chief executive wanted the company 'to be there'. Too often, Web sites are built without a clear and realistic objective in mind. As a result, the Web is littered with ill-conceived sites that nobody bothers to visit or maintain.

There are plenty of much-visited sites that have no obvious commercial intent. They are there for information or just for fun, with no prospect of making any money. But most businesses need a financial justification for their investment and must find a way to use the new medium to gain commercial advantage.

The first question to ask when planning an online marketing campaign is, how does the Web fit into the overall marketing plan? Web activity should be treated as an integral part of a communication strategy, as shown in Figure 5.1. For maximum effectiveness the message should be consistent with, build on or complement that given in other media. By adopting an integrated approach across all aspects of communication, a greater penetration and more effective build-up of impact can be achieved.

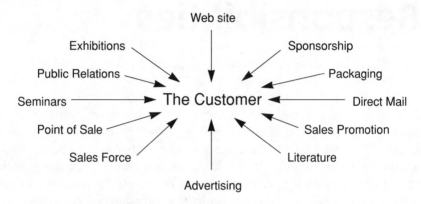

Figure 5.1 *Building a consistent message*

For example, the BBC's official 'EastEnders' Web site (www. bbc.co.uk/eastenders) is part of an advertising campaign for the TV soap opera. A comprehensive Q&A section enables viewers to find out more details, vote for their favourite 'EastEnders' moments, and look at scenes from Albert Square in RealVideo at any time of day or night. You can tour the Square and hear what the residents think of their lives.

BUILDING A RELATIONSHIP WITH THE CONSUMER

One of the great opportunities of Web interactivity is that it allows marketers to reach precisely targeted customers and to build a relationship with them. It is increasingly hard to win market share from competitors, and a brand or company's customer base is likely to be constantly eroded. It is argued that building stronger relationships with users increases their predisposition to remain loyal, participate in promotions and to buy the brand.

'One-to-one' and 'relationship marketing' are buzzwords of the late 1990s. The concepts are based on developing a better understanding of consumers as individuals, and building on that understanding to establish a relationship with them. This can be used to identify the most valuable customers and to build loyalty.

Some groups of consumers can be targeted with precision on the Web, and the message can be customized for the individual. This means that a brand is no longer restricted to one message for everyone, but can tailor different communications for different segments of the target audience. This allows the relevance of the brand to the consumer to be maximized.

One-to-one marketing guru Don Peppers cites Amazon as one of the best examples of one-to-one marketing. Figures in early 1999 show that Amazon customers have a 64 per cent repeat visit rate, far higher than that of conventional bookstores. Amazon customizes itself to each individual who visits its pages. You enter your name, address and credit card details once, and from then on can buy any book just by clicking a single *icon* on the screen. The computer system watches what you buy to judge your tastes and then starts offering titles it thinks may appeal to you. The relationship starts with the first transaction and works on hooking you as a customer for life. Don Peppers says:

> It creates a learning relationship that gets smarter and smarter the more you use it. The reason this is a compelling model is that it makes the customer more loyal to you. I buy books from Amazon and, in all probability, I could get them cheaper somewhere else. But why should I bother? I know Amazon, it's easy to use, and to buy somewhere else I would have to go through the business of entering my address and credit card details again. As long as Amazon is good to me as a customer, I'm theirs.

However, it is important to keep things in perspective. It is not realistic for every product and service to expect to strike up a relationship with its target audience. Consumers can only manage a finite number of online relationships, and these are likely to be reserved for those brands and services that are of high interest or offer real benefits.

COLLECTING USER DATA

The Internet has given one-to-one marketing a boost, as the inter-active nature of the Web helps the marketer to collect individual data, and to use that data to establish a relevant dialogue.

Just as consumers do not benefit from striking up a relationship with every brand on the Web, so brands will find that relationships with some customers are more important than relationships with others. A database can be very helpful in identifying the most valu-able users; for example, 20 per cent of a brand's users may account for 80 per cent of turnover. This type of knowledge can be used to improve the targeting of messages and use of resources.

The key to getting good, accurate information from a Web user is to make it a quick and easy process. Data can be collected in a number of ways:

▧ online registration forms or guest-books;
▧ questions contained within the site content, for example to allow access to a particular area of the site;
▧ online surveys and customer feedback;
▧ information supplied by users while making a transaction;
▧ tracking user activities.

Users may only be prepared to volunteer personal information if they perceive value in what they receive in return. This value may lie in the site content, or the enhanced service they receive as a result of customizing the site. Otherwise, tracking user activities can be done anonymously with the use of *cookies*, which are pieces of information stored in a text file on a user's computer.

In the past, most databases were based on the transactions made by consumers. This has its limitations: how often have you received a personalized letter where your name is spelt incorrectly, your sex changed and the product information totally irrelevant to your lifestyle? But new data management marketing techniques (such as *data warehousing* and *data mining*) help marketers to store and analyse large amounts of complex data obtained from a variety of sources. With information supplied from the Web already in digital format, details can be loaded into databases where software can search for similarities, differences and patterns that can feed into marketing initiatives. Lifestyle and lifestage data can help to give insight into an individual's hierarchy of decision making, greatly increasing the potential to build a relationship with the consumer.

For example, Unilever, Kimberley-Clark and Cadbury have formed an alliance in the UK to build a joint relationship marketing database. It draws its data from the multiple consumer contacts that these companies have between them, and is used to develop relationship marketing programmes for their brands and to investigate opportunities. Web visitors and promotions provide a useful additional source of information for the database.

PERSONALIZATION

With the help of Web server technology, the information from databases can be used to customize Web pages and personalize messages. This is particularly useful in cases where a product or service has more than one target market, or several different products and services are on offer. Personalizing the Web experience can mean anything from providing a personalized home page that gives users the information they selected on their previous visit(s), to a full service system tracking preferences, interactions, purchase history and giving recommendations.

It is important to remember that these 'personalized' interactions are all with a computer rather than a human, and are most appropriate for high volume repetitive interactions where a computer can be programed to perform the task efficiently. But electronically generated standard responses that are clumsily executed can undermine brand credibility or even cause offence, and it is more difficult to replace the type of face-to-face sales service expected in some categories.

Some attempts are being made to add a human touch to personalized services. For example, online clothes shop Boo.com (www.boo.com) has introduced a virtual shop assistant, inspired by Tomb Raider's Lara Croft. Ms Boo, an electronic 'sartorial mistress', speaks six languages including American English. In American she gushes more and says 'pants' and 'sneakers' instead of 'trousers' and 'trainers'. She is the typical shop assistant with attitude, getting bored if you are too slow browsing the virtual shelves of her store, giving advice on outfits and suggesting other outfits to match your taste.

Web site personalization allows users to build profiles based on their own choices. The registration process itself gives people a sense that they are in control of choosing their preferences. However, it is important to let your customers opt-in and opt-out of the personalization process. Nothing frustrates an online user more than being forced to provide information to a Web site in order to participate. The chances are they will either go away or give false information.

SETTING OBJECTIVES

Just like all other parts of a marketing strategy, a Web campaign needs to be developed against clear and realistic objectives that can be quantified and measured over a specified period of time. These will be influenced by the competitive context, target consumer and the nature of the product or service. Some objectives can be met very well via the Web, others may be better pursued through other media.

Objectives may, for example, be to increase awareness; build brand image; increase sales; generate loyalty; capture user data; or reduce costs.

To increase awareness

Research company Millward Brown conducted a quantified test in 1996/7 with the objective of measuring the impact of a single ad *banner* exposure on brand awareness. The three brands tested included a men's apparel brand, a telecommunications brand and a technology company. The test found that awareness was significantly greater among the banner-exposed (test) group than the non-exposed (control) group. Exposure to the advertising banners alone increased brand awareness from 12 per cent to 20 per cent in the banner-exposed group.

The Web's reach is, however, still small relative to traditional broadcast media. For standardized products it is still difficult to beat the broadcast media as an effective means of building awareness with a mass target audience.

To build brand image

In the early days, simply associating a brand with the Internet would add contemporary values. Teen-focused brands can reinforce their up-to-date credentials in cyberspace. The ability of the Web to store large amounts of data and to respond to individual questions also makes it a suitable means to educate consumers and to improve corporate PR, for example on environmental, trading and human resource policies.

The Web can extend the definition of a brand beyond the product, so that consumers can 'live the brand'. Many brand owners are creating Web sites in an attempt to add to the 'brand experience', hosting chat rooms, discussion forums and entertainment for their target audience.

Advertising executions on the Web are limited by bandwidth. Without broadband capacity, the Web still lacks the visual and emotional appeal of the full motion video, high-quality art and music so often used in advertising to build brand imagery. This and the relatively limited audience exposure make the Web less appropriate for mass-market brand building than for providing detailed information about brands that consumers already recognize from other media.

Increasingly, having a Web presence of some kind is becoming a prerequisite to maintain credibility for hi-tech companies, designers and agencies. It is not just a question of what benefit the Web site can bring, but also how much credibility is lost by not being there.

The effect on image can be negative as well as positive. A badly designed Web site or one that is not updated frequently can undermine the brand image. Services that are not properly resourced (for example e-mail contacts for queries and customer service lines) cause more frustration and disillusionment than if they were not there.

To increase sales

The Web can provide extensive information about a product. It can be used to attract sales inquiries (which may then be followed up by traditional means), to link potential buyers to a site where the product can be bought online, and to act as a trading post where customers can buy things online.

Sales incentives can be offered through online promotional offers, prize draws and competitions. Low-involvement and impulse product promotional sites can stimulate brand trial through free samples and coupons that are requested online and either sent by post or printed off the computer for redemption at leading supermarkets.

The Web is a potentially powerful new channel of distribution. However, online transactions require extensive knowledge of databases, security and the laws dealing with financial transactions.

To generate loyalty

Consumers who actively decide to visit a Web site are likely to be receptive to the brand offer. They can be targeted with free samples, online coupons, regular competitions and promotional offers with less wastage than is common for other direct marketing campaigns. A high proportion of Web site visitors are likely to have bought the brand already, so offers will tend to reward existing users rather than increase penetration.

People tend to seek advice and information from brands and organizations that they know and trust. Consumers are becoming increasingly cynical about the commercial motives of brands and are likely to turn to independent authorities for objective information. Not every brand can expect to build a relationship with its consumers.

To capture user data

Interactivity allows a two-way flow of information. A Web site may be used as a means to collect data on consumers. Information collected may be used to customize and personalize the visitor's Web experience, and utilized offline for traditional marketing activities, or to sell targeted advertising space.

Too often, Web sites ask for personal information just for the sake of it and then fail to do anything with it. From the consumer point of view, this can be very disappointing. From the brand point of view, providing a truly personal service of value to the individual requires ongoing resources.

To reduce costs

The automation of ordering, invoicing and customer services can cut down on paperwork. Businesses can save money by offering online order tracking so that customers can keep a check on the status of their order without having to call customer services. This can help to reduce staff levels and overheads (see the Dell case study in Chapter 4).

For businesses that operate on constant change (in product line and prices), a Web catalogue is cheaper to update and distribute than originating and printing new material each time. Once the content of an online catalogue is created, there are no incremental costs for distributing additional copies. Image quality may be reduced, but unlimited information can be provided and pricing updated as often as necessary.

In some instances, the Web may provide a means to cheap market research through online surveys and consumer panels. Some companies hold focus groups in chat rooms, reducing the cost of traditional groups (travel) and allowing access to foreign markets.

Unilever

Unilever in the US has conducted tests using Lipton Recipe Secrets brand to explore the opportunity to build relationships between the brand and the consumer on the Web. The tests were run on the @Home network, which is a high-speed Internet cable connection to the home. The @Home service has broadband capacity and delivers the Internet to the TV, so the quality of video images is significantly better than on a PC monitor. It also has the advantage for test purposes of being a controlled environment for market research, as it can only be accessed by subscribers.

Lipton Recipe Secrets hosted a food Web site where consumers could find more than 6,000 recipe ideas provided by the Lipton Kitchens, and also learn about basic cooking skills with short, easy-to-follow videos (see Figure 5.2). Quantitative market research was conducted among 3,404 @Home subscribers, divided into three groups: those who were not exposed to any brand communication, those who were exposed to banner advertising only, and those who had visited the Web site.

The results demonstrated the impact that a Web site and advertising can have on brand image, loyalty, and also frequency of use and purchase intent:

Figure 5.2 *A new recipe and cooking tip every day*

■ Exposure to banners alone caused the unaided brand awareness of Lipton as a food brand to increase from 3 per cent to 5 per cent, and exposure to the Recipe Secrets Web site in the last three months led to an increase to 13 per cent.
■ Lipton brand image indicators improved after a visit to the site:

'Expert in providing meal ideas I can use' rose from 36 per cent to 67 per cent, and 'Made by a company with innovative ideas' from 33 per cent to 60 per cent.

▩ Of all the consumers who visited the site, 62 per cent downloaded or printed a recipe. Of these, 78 per cent actually made the recipe, of which 80 per cent made it with Recipe Secrets as an ingredient. Twenty-nine per cent actually went to a store to buy the product to make the recipe, which nets out at 11 per cent of all site visitors.

ROLES AND RESPONSIBILITIES

It is important to make it clear who is responsible for managing Web initiatives and incorporating them into the marketing programme.

Early initiatives for exploring and employing Web technologies often come from the IT department, which has the awareness of new technologies and the ability to make them work. However, in most cases it is appropriate for sales and marketing rather than IT to take overall responsibility for setting objectives, briefing the implementation and evaluating the results of a Web campaign. IT takes on a support role, informing sales and marketing of what is available on the technology frontier, helping them to think through the opportunities and challenges of every new technology, and providing technical support.

For example, at Bank of America (www.BankAmerica.com) a team reporting directly to the head of the retail bank manages the online banking Web site. This team includes technical specialists but is headed by a banker with strong marketing experience. Also included are legal, public relations and communications experts.

In order to get the best from the Web and to keep pace with rapid technological change, marketers and their agencies need to communicate with IT people in a way they never have before. This can throw up some strange new relationships. Managers may sit there scratching their heads wondering why the IT director is in a client pitch – 'Shouldn't he be downstairs making the laptops work?' However, the balance of this relationship is important to

maintain, letting the IT department pursue exciting new technological developments that are unintelligible to most mortals, while
marketing takes responsibility for briefing and monitoring site
content.

The results can be significant, as the 1998 Information Technology FT Business Web Site Awards found:

> This was the year that big companies took their Web sites away from
> their IT departments and gave them to sales and marketing. And,
> boy, does it show. This year's best sites really work as a way of doing
> business. Where once Web pages were designed by geeks for geeks
> who would see something cool and peer into the source code to see
> how it was done, now they have been designed to make buyers peer
> into their wallets for their credit cards.

Responsibility for Web activity is by no means universally
assumed by sales and marketing. Even in some marketing-led
multinational companies, marketing directors have been heard to
admit that they have never even looked at their Web site.
However, one suspects that the excuse that 'it cost peanuts' and is
'only tactical' may simply be another way of saying, 'I don't
understand this new medium, and am ashamed to admit to my
team that I have no idea how to surf the Web.' This can result in
responsibility being delegated to managers with little marketing
experience and to the IT department. No other part of the
marketing budget would be handed over in such a cavalier
fashion!

THINK GLOBAL?

The Web is potentially a global medium. Although penetration still
varies widely by country, usage is growing exponentially. Once a
site is placed on the Web, it can be accessed in any country in the
world. This has significant management implications for international brands and businesses.

Some multinational brand owners respond with one universal
Web site, so realizing the obvious advantages in consistency of
message and sharing the cost of generating content between
countries. Companies such as Coca-Cola (www.cocacola.com),
where the company name and the brand name are the same,

combine corporate and brand elements and control them in one Web site. Coca-Cola gives financial results, promotes the corporate mission, and provides entertainment for consumers to enhance the brand's fun image, all within the same site.

However, it is not always practical – or politically popular – for decentralized businesses that 'think global and act local' to consolidate their Web presence globally. For example, despite a common name and livery across its products, and a commitment to 'master brand' advertising, Cadbury runs separate chocolate sites in the UK (www.cadbury.co.uk and www.cadburylearningzone.co.uk), Australia (www.cadbury.com.au), Ireland (www.cadbury.ie), Poland (www.cadbury.com.pl), Canada (www.cadbury.chocolate.ca) and New Zealand (www.cadbury.co.nz). These are in addition to the dedicated Creme egg, Crunchie, Boost, Astros and Bassetts sites. Some attempts are being made to coordinate and share material under common themes (the 'Land of Cadbury' and 'Great Bunny') but control of Web initiatives is not centralized.

Unilever maintains its traditionally low corporate profile, preferring to launch different Web sites for different markets, and allowing the possibility of more than one Web site per brand (for example, www.mentadent.com for the US market, and www.mentadent.it for Italian consumers). At the last count, there were over 40 promotional brand sites in addition to the corporate Web site. But the approach adopted by the European detergent division of Unilever reconciles the characteristics of an intrinsically international medium with local management needs. A multilingual Home Page (www.clothes-care.com) is the common point of entry for all the European detergent brands, and visitors then choose their language and link through to relevant country sites. Product information remains consistent but the local business units run local promotions and services.

Cadbury and Unilever are not the only multinational companies to have left control of Web activity to local management to date. P&G maintain 17 'informational and entertaining sites dedicated to you and your home', each with a different Web address but linked to a P&G corporate site (www.pg.com). The Nestlé network lists 31 sites. However, if the proportion of the marketing budget spent online increases from current levels of around 1 per cent to a significant proportion of the total, you can be sure that the benefits of exercising greater central control will be explored.

CHECKLIST

Make sure that the appropriate level of knowledge and skills exists within the marketing department, and arrange training where required:

■ Numerous training programmes and seminars are advertised in the marketing and business press, and other suggestions can be sought by typing in relevant word strings such as 'Internet + UK + marketing + training' on to the search engines.

■ It may be that the most senior personnel with the best strategic skills and experience of the market are the least confident with the new technology. Find ways to give them first-hand Web surfing experience, and to introduce them to the relevant marketing issues without having to suffer unnecessary jargon and technological detail. One-to-one online training sessions using relevant category demonstrations and market/competitor activity reviews can be helpful.

■ For marketing teams with a range of different skill levels, team sessions and workshops can be useful as a means both to ensure a common knowledge base and to facilitate the development of a strategy. Organizational challenges can also be addressed.

See 'Training' in Useful Contacts and Further Reading, page 155.

Chapter glossary

Banner   Advertisement placed on a Web site to flag information. Can be a simple message or moving images.

Cookie   A very small text file placed on a user's hard drive by a Web Page server. It works as an identification card that can only be read by the server that placed it. The purpose of a cookie is to tell the server when a user returns to that Web page, so that the browser can recall personal details and registration for products and services, and show the information requested.

Data mining   Identifying commercially useful patterns or relationships in databases or other computer repositories through the use of advanced statistical tools.

Data warehouse   A database that can access all of a company's information. Data may be stored on several different computers in different databases, all of which the warehouse can retrieve and analyse.

Icon   A graphic image used to represent a topic or category of information on a Web page. Clicking on the icon may provide a hypertext link to that page.

One-to-one marketing   One-to-one or one-to-few communication with a customized message for each individual or narrowly targeted market. This contrasts with mass marketing where a common message is communicated to all.

Relationship marketing   Developing a deeper understanding of the consumer through knowledge and experience. The consumer is the focus of marketing efforts, and communication becomes a dialogue through which loyalty can be built.

6

Developing a Web Campaign

Building a full-blown Web site is not the only way to establish a presence on the Web. Advertising and sponsorship can provide an effective alternative for a Web campaign, and pass the burden of attracting the target audience and providing a continuous flow of up-to-date information and relevant material to specialist content providers.

TYPES OF WEB SITE

A few years ago, most Internet campaigns involved little more than a hastily constructed corporate Web site, designed simply to establish a presence in this new medium. More complex and sophisticated sites designed to promote products and services and to encourage electronic trading have since proliferated. Different types of Web campaign may be appropriate for a company's various publics; it is not always possible to appeal to everyone at the same time. So, defining exactly who is the intended recipient of the message is vital. Figure 6.1 shows a number of different target audiences.

The broad categories of Web site commonly available are summarized below.

Content sites are those that use a service, information and/or entertainment to attract and retain an audience in order to

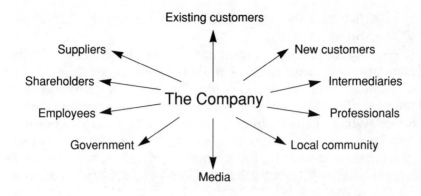

Figure 6.1 *Different target audiences*

sell advertising or subscriptions. Popular content sites include search engines and browsers (eg, Yahoo! and Netscape), media owners (TV, newspapers and magazines), and event sites (eg, football).

For example, the Time Warner Pathfinder (www.pathfinder. com) site carries extensive content from its magazine, TV, music and film divisions which include *Time, Life, People* and *Fortune* magazines, CNN, Warner Brothers, Warner Bros records, *Entertainment Weekly*. It attracts a large, highly educated audience and earns revenue through selling advertising packages on its site. ThePathfinder marketing department helps advertisers to create online content and advertising.

Community sites offer a range of services such as links to virtual shopping malls, information services, career opportunities, community workers, bulletin boards and places where visitors can just hang out and chat. Revenue comes from advertising and commission or royalties on sales made through the site.

For example, one of the first community sites, appearing in 1994, was Bianca's Shack (www.bianca.com). Billed as 'the alternative online community', it offers a range of 'shacks' on different topics. Visitors to Bianca's Smut Shack get a map of an apartment, and by clicking on any of the rooms they can join in with the activities in that area, including ongoing bulletin board discussions and chat sessions with other people hanging out there at that moment. In the kitchen, for instance, people enter recipes in the cookbook. In the living room they post erotic poetry. In the bedroom they log dreams they had last night into Bianca's dream book... expect 'adult-natured content'!

The biggest online community today is America Online (www.aol.com), with over 14 million members worldwide. The AOL concept was developed before the arrival of the World Wide Web and all AOL members pay a monthly subscription for the service (which includes Internet access). AOL makes a concerted effort to please advertisers by enabling them to reach a women-only target more easily, for example through a new 'women's channel' that will direct subscribers to certain health, parenting and career Web sites.

GeoCities (www.geocities.com) relies on individuals or 'home-steaders' (mainly US-based) to create their own Web site and then place it on GeoCities in one of the 41 themed neighbour-hoods. If you have a site dedicated to the environment, for example, you can place your Web site in the 'Rain Forest' amongst other sites of similar interest. GeoCities owns and sells all of the advertising space. GeoCities is one of the top five destination sites.

Promotional sites exist for the purpose of promoting products, increasing brand awareness and brand loyalty, and developing a dialogue with the consumer. Few promotional sites derive direct income from advertising or subscriptions, although some offer online sales of products and related merchandise.

For example, P&G's new Olean brand promises consumers the opportunity to reduce their fat intake and still enjoy the taste and texture of their favourite snacks, thanks to the development of Olestra. This is claimed to be the first fat replacement to replicate all of the properties of fat without contributing calories or fat to the diet. The Olean promotional Web site (www.olean.com) explains how, giving professionals, journalists and other interested parties access to a technical database of information on Olestra.

Transaction sites offer users the opportunity to buy products and services over the Internet without having to visit a shop or agent. These may be transactions involving the transfer of infor-mation and provision of a service, or ordering goods for distribu-tion by traditional methods.

For example, choosing the right mobile phone package is a complex and traumatic experience requiring an informed and objective comparison of the alternatives available, which can be provided as effectively by a computer as a busy sales assistant. The Carphone Warehouse's Web site (www.carphone.co.uk) leads potential customers through the maze of different services, tariffs and mobile phones available, invites individuals to input their specifications and recommends the best solutions. The package can then be ordered through the online shopping service.

An increasingly popular means of buying and selling on the Web is through auction sites. Online trading pioneer eBay (www.ebay.com) has developed a Web-based community in which individuals are brought together to buy and sell personal items such as antiques, coins, collectibles, computers, memorabilia and toys. The QXL (commonly known as quixell or quick-sell) Web site (www.qxl.com) arranges auctions between consumers and business-to-consumers for a range of new and second-hand products and services. Auction sites can be used by businesses to get the best price for end-of-line goods or where there is spare capacity: for example travel, holiday and entertainment companies sell spare tickets to the highest bidder on sites such as QXL or Lastminute (www.lastminute.com).

Corporate sites are used for corporate communications, to promote company data, policies and recruitment information as well as brand values. In the early days of the Web, company Web sites were often little more than an electronic annual report, but the potential of the medium both as an extended sales and marketing arm and a powerful way to interact with customers, shareholders and investors is now being realized. Analysts' presentations delivered via the Internet can influence share value, and the AGM or corporate videos can now be embedded into corporate sites.

For example, the Arcadia retail group (previously Burtons) experimented with a live online chat session for the opening of TopShop at Oxford Circus, when 250 customers wanted to talk online to pop-star Billie Piper. The same format was used subsequently for a question and answer session for journalists with the Arcadia CEO (www.principles.co.uk).

CHOOSING THE RIGHT ROUTE

There are several different ways to establish a presence on the Web:

▦ develop your own *destination Web site*;
▦ create a *micro site* that can be hosted on a content site;
▦ place advertising on a content site;
▦ sponsor someone else's site.

These are shown in Figure 6.2. The first step is to consider whether it is feasible to create a destination site that users want to visit, or whether it is better to utilize the power of someone else's content that already attracts the desired target audience.

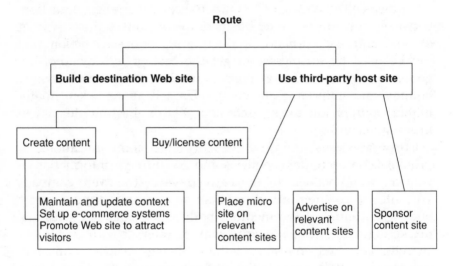

Figure 6.2 *Establishing a Web presence*

Products that can be sold online and shipped economically or delivered digitally (such as music, tickets, books or software) can use a destination site to support everything from product information through to post-sales support. Complex products such as computers and cars can use a Web site to help customers check specifications, configure their purchase and get product support online. Dealing with sales queries, orders and customer services online can cut costs.

But for products that cannot offer online sales and services it may be easier to buy into popular content on a site that has already generated an audience than it is to create new content.

Micro sites are like mini Web sites. They can consist of one or several pages communicating a promotion or simple brand message, but rather than being placed in their own unique location on the Web they are distributed across media sites. This can in many instances be done for a fraction of the cost of building and maintaining a full Web site.

If the campaign objective is to raise awareness or build brand equity, then it may be more effective to advertise on a content site already frequented by the target audience. Advertising on a content site can be stand-alone, link through to a temporary promotional site or to a permanent brand Web site.

For example, Levi Strauss has been one of the leading pioneers on the Web. Its campaign includes a destination Web site (costing a rumoured US $3 million) and a separate online advertising campaign aimed at raising awareness among the youth market. Its 'I-candy' (as in 'sweets for your eyes'!) campaign places icons and banners on content sites: when clicked on, they download animated graphics on to a micro site before taking you back to wherever you were originally. One advertising execution has a small round porthole, through which you can see a mermaid swim past. Clicking on the advertisement brings up a multimedia game, in which users have to rescue a sailor from the bottom of the sea without being eaten by sharks and various other underwater beasts. There is no link on to the Levi's site or any attempt to sell jeans, as the objective is simply brand awareness and image.

Online sponsorship is one of the fastest-growing areas of Web advertising. Just as product placement in films and TV programmes and programme sponsorship can prove an effective alternative to traditional advertising, so the Web offers scope for sponsored programming. Sponsorships of online content are much like event sponsorships: the hope is that users will associate the content with the advertiser.

For example, Carling sponsors the UK Premier Football League site (www.fa-premier.com; see Figure 6.3) as part of its overall brand sponsorship programme. The official Web site is heavily branded with Carling throughout. The Football and Press Associations provide up-to-date content including pre-match, half- and full-time match reports and action pictures. For those who register, a discussion group for each football club provides fans with the opportunity to discuss their team.

Figure 6.3 *Carling sponsorship of the FA Premier League*

Sponsoring a site allows the brand owner to introduce not just the logo and brand style but also advertising, promotions and *advertorial* material on to the parent site.

For example, ParentTime (www.parenttime.com) is a joint venture between Time Warner's *Parenting* magazine in the US (which provides all content), and P&G (which has made a US $1 million multi-year advertising commitment). The site provides personalized information on child development, health and medical information, entertainment and activities, relationships, family finance, news and events. P&G regularly runs advertising and promotions for brands such as Pampers and Tide on ParentTime, and (probably) has some input into editorial features.

This type of commercial alliance and sponsorship arrangement gives rise to concern in some quarters that the increasing commercialization of the Web is in danger of undermining its value as a serious source of online information. The line between editorial and advertising can become blurred, and many users are likely to be put off by advertising masquerading as fact.

Creating a destination site, micro site, advertising and sponsorship are not mutually exclusive options, and many Web campaigns are built on a combination of routes. Destination Web sites need to be advertised online to announce their presence, and brands wanting to build awareness may place attention-getting advertisements independent of their Web site.

Mentadent
www.mentadent.com

The original US Mentadent toothpaste Web site contained extensive information on oral care targeted at consumers, dentists and oral hygiene professionals. The problem was that very few people saw a reason to visit the site.

Mentadent's objective was to develop more loyal consumers by establishing a direct relationship with them, so they set about designing a more effective Web campaign. First of all, the main Web site was redesigned to reflect more closely the consumer needs identified in research. Then Mentadent banner advertising was placed on health-oriented media content sites; see Figure 6.4a. Consumers who clicked on the banner were transported to a micro site that engaged them in an interactive story of how Mentadent works. This served to educate users and potential new users while capturing data such as demographics, brand usage and permission to re-contact. The consumer was invited to complete a form to receive a Mentadent toothpaste sample and US $0.55 coupon by post, before finally linking into the full Mentadent site; see Figure 6.4b.

Over 65,000 requests for samples were received, 80 per cent of which were from Mentadent non-users. Seventy per cent of those responding gave Mentadent permission to re-contact them.

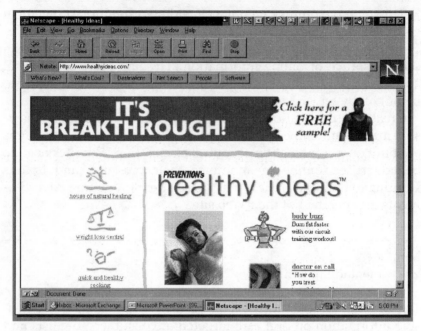

Figure 6.4a *Clicking the animated banner on this health site...*

Figure 6.4b *... leads to a pop-up Mentadent sample request form*

ORGANIZATIONAL IMPLICATIONS

Starting a Web-based campaign places new requirements on the organization. Before embarking on any of the options above, it is worth considering the resources and skill sets required, and the impact this will have on the organization.

Building and maintaining a Web site entails taking on responsibility not only for creating the brand message but also for designing and organizing the context or environment in which it is published, updating the content, hosting the site and attracting visitors. This requires skills and resources beyond conventional brand management, and a *Webmaster* or *Webmistress* may be needed to supervise the smooth running of the site. So, for example, the marketing department manages the marketing Web site at Levi Strauss (www.levi.com) with support from a Webmaster.

An effective Web site needs to be constantly updated and refreshed in order to compete in what is a very dynamic environment. The problem with expecting the marketing team or agency to create content is that this is not a core skill for either party. A professional-looking Web site is thirsty for new material and new technology, and the burden of attracting the target audience and providing a continuous flow of up-to-date content is sometimes better borne by specialists. This is one of the reasons why brand owners are increasingly buying or licensing content from the likes of the Press Association, established publishers and specialist content providers.

Placing advertising or sponsorship on relevant content sites is a more familiar role for marketing and agencies, which are used to designing and producing brand communication material and buying media space. But some companies that have launched Web initiatives working with their traditional agencies report that the experience has been disappointing. Traditional creatives may think more about the 'look' of advertising than the interactive experience that consumers expect, and some argue that a natural prejudice against the medium risks becoming a self-fulfilling prophecy. However, attitudes to the new medium are changing: traditional agencies are realizing that even if it is not the area where clients are spending the most money at the moment, it's the thing most clients want to talk about. When they see the client interest and witness other agencies getting in on the act, they realize that to retain their position as the voice of authority they need to know about it and get involved.

Even so, creative input may need to be sought from outside traditional advertising agencies. Web creative work has tended to pass to the rising new media agencies, which generally show better understanding of the ways in which an active Web experience differs from the passive nature of TV. There is a plethora of advertising agencies, PR consultancies and design and publishing houses all rushing to take advantage of the new media opportunities. Note that if Web creative work is taken away from the traditional agency, this breaks down the idea of a 'one-stop-shop' for all communication solutions and puts the onus of being the guardian of communication consistency back on to marketing.

When assessing a new agency, it is worth paying particular attention to:

▧ Stability. Since the explosion of activity on the Web, agencies, firms and consultants have leapt on the bandwagon but in many cases the experience they bring is quite thin. The Web is a new medium, but Web developers who have not been in the business for at least three years are still considered relatively inexperienced. There have been some high-profile Internet agency failures, so check financial credentials too.
▧ Track record. Look for a list of long-term clients and feedback on whether work has been developed on time and within budget. Use an agency that can already demonstrate that it understands your business and has competence in the design features you are likely to require.
▧ Expertise. Check that there is a good balance between technical and commercial expertise. The marketing brief should drive the choice of technology, not vice versa. And check where the skills reside: many PR and marketing companies claim Web expertise but actually farm out Web development to sub-contractors, which means that you pay for the privilege of passing work through a company that knows little or nothing about Web development.

Companies that are committed to using the Web as an increasingly important part of their marketing strategy may decide to develop knowledge of and expertise in interactive media in a centre of excellence within their own organization.

Interactive Brand Centres

Unilever is setting up dedicated Interactive Brand Centres (IBCs) to provide a strategic framework and promote cross-learning in the key areas of marketing and retailing its products through the Internet.

The first IBC (based in New York) consists of a multi-functional team of more than a dozen professionals on four continents. The team members have varied expertise including marketing, market research, interactive advertising, customer development, IT publishing, database management and e-commerce. A second IBC opened in Amsterdam in 1999 to spearhead efforts in Europe, and a third is planned for Singapore.

The IBC serves as an internal consultancy, setting up tests, evaluating new ways to use the medium and disseminating best practice. While Unilever's brand managers are ultimately responsible for the success of their products in the marketplace, the IBC helps to explore new platforms for growth, develop appropriate strategies and to choose the agencies with which they can best implement them.

The IBC has also built a database of more than 10 million Unilever consumers through Unilever's branded Web sites and free customer service numbers. This will be a resource for relationship marketing and cross-branding initiatives; for example, a US Ragu customer who has expressed an interest in recipes from Ragu may also receive beauty advice from Dove soap, or laundry tips from Wisk detergent.

Unilever believes that the way forward is through alliances and partnerships, and has forged strategic marketing relationships with:

▓ AOL;
▓ Microsoft Network;
▓ NetGrocer;
▓ @Home (cable Internet access and content provider).

It is through working with these partners that Unilever hopes to build innovative programmes and interactive advertising executions, and to get exclusive rights to sponsor and place promotions in relevant content areas.

CHECKLIST

▩ Decide whether you need a destination Web site and, if so, how you plan to sustain it in terms of both content and resource.

▩ Before developing the campaign, define what kind of expertise and IT infrastructure (particularly for transaction sites) is likely to be required and assess whether this is available in-house/through current agencies.

▩ If you decide to outsource design and creative work, consider using a new media agency.

Chapter glossary

Advertorial Brand-sponsored messages and related editorial placed on an existing content site.

Content site A term used to describe a site able to attract a large number of visitors simply through the utility of and interest in the information it provides.

Destination Web site A Web site that uses information, entertainment and production values to pull users in and generate repeat visits.

Micro site A cluster of pages developed by a brand and hosted by a content site.

Webmaster/mistress The person responsible for creating and maintaining a Web site. Often responsible for responding to e-mail, ensuring the site is operating properly, creating and updating Web pages, and maintaining the overall structure and design of the site.

7

Developing a Web Site

Do it right or don't do it at all. There are many under-resourced and badly executed Web sites that attract little traffic and are at best a waste of money and may even harm the brand. In the dynamic world of the Web, a site needs to be carefully constructed, constantly updated and actively promoted, or consumers will get bored and go elsewhere.

STAGES OF DEVELOPMENT

There is serious competition on the Web these days. An estimated 1.5 million new sites are being launched globally every day, but up to 50 per cent of traffic goes to the top 500 sites. In order to stand out in the busy online marketplace it is important to offer something as good as or better than that which is already available, and a point of difference.

A Web site must have a clear purpose and consumer proposition, and be well publicized in order to attract visitors in the dynamic Web environment. It is not enough to provide a once-off interest site: it needs to be updated, maintained and refreshed in order to get visitors to return again and again.

The stages of development for a Web site are:

- create the *content*;
- design the look and feel;
- programme the content;
- choose a *host*.

Some aspects may be handled in-house, but marketers with no previous experience of the Web are advised to outsource much of the work. The quality of the brief given to external consultants and new media agencies and the way in which it is monitored are likely to have a significant impact on the resulting Web site.

CREATING CONTENT

Conventional Web wisdom (if that is not a contradiction in terms) says that 'Content is King'. The best way to generate traffic and get users to return to a site regularly is to provide useful and interesting content. The context or online environment also plays an important role in generating loyalty and building a relationship. Useful information can be presented in an enjoyable context that offers entertainment too.

The hook

Consumers need a compelling reason to visit a Web site in the first place. Where interest in a brand or business is high, the provision of product information or the opportunity to buy online may provide a sufficient 'reason why'. But in other categories, a hook is needed to attract attention in a way that is relevant to potential users. This might, for example, be newsworthy information, an offer or incentive such as a competition, discount, sample or freebie, entertainment in a game, access to an online community of interest or shopping.

For example, Card4you (www.card4you.com) provides a wide range of entertaining active (video and audio) greetings cards, which includes Paris scenes with fireworks exploding to the sound of the Marseillaise for Bastille Day. The idea is that the sender picks or designs a virtual card and hits the 'send' button. This triggers an e-mail to the intended recipient, with a hyperlink to the Web site where the card can be viewed. The recipient has to go and collect his or her card from the Web site, where they can also design their own card to send to someone else. Once visitors are enticed to the site to collect the card and message from the sender, they are invited to sign up for a number of information services.

Sites that aim to capture consumer data should link these efforts with the 'hook' mechanism, as people are more inclined to enter personal data if they can see a benefit or gain a reward.

Generating repeat visits

Having got the user's attention, it is important for building loyalty to provide content that will have them coming back again and again. The topic must, however, 'fit' the brand image: brands that try to entice visitors to their own Web site with entertaining material unrelated to the brand run the risk of confusing consumers about the brand focus and values. If a brand is not associated with sport, why should users trust it to supply content in that area? If no suitable hook can be found it may be worth reconsidering the decision to create a separate site.

For example, Pepsi (www.pepsi.co.uk) has launched a music portal, aiming to become the main source of music news on the Web. It gets content from a number of music sources and a music-orientated search facility from search engine Lycos. Pepsi claims that there is an established link to music via the brand, which has in the past sponsored Michael Jackson and the Spice Girls.

Web site owners are increasingly turning to third parties for help in providing the sort of up-to-date content that the environment demands. The challenge of creating interesting content on a regular basis is outside the scope and experience of most businesses, and demands huge resources. The alternative is to buy content from the likes of the Press Association and media owners who specialize in providing and updating content on an ongoing basis.

But creating or buying original content can be expensive and some sites have found that users are equally happy creating their own. Just like the TV craze for so-called 'docusoaps', people can be endlessly fascinated by the opportunity to share the reality of their everyday lives and opinions with others in chat rooms and online communities.

DESIGN AND BRANDING

The 'look' and 'feel' of a Web site influence the visitor's experience. A well-designed site that is easy to use is more likely to attract repeat business than one that is complex and impenetrable.

Structure

Web visitors are free to move about a Web site in any direction they choose. They do not have to explore it in a linear fashion or follow the route recommended by the owner. A site must therefore be easy to navigate. The golden rule of good site design is: 'architecture precedes aesthetics'. A clear structure and carefully constructed links between pages help visitors to find their way around.

Many successful sites are organized around a central theme or metaphor. Where the site is complex or varied, this helps users to plan their visit and find their way around. For example, visitors to the Ragu site (www.eat.com; see Figure 7.1) are invited into the world of 'Mama's Cucina' where they can meet Mama and watch her present information about gourmet Italian cooking and culture. The site is presented as an Italian house, and visitors can click from the kitchen to the dining room or family room to explore various topics. The concept is maintained throughout the site, visually and in the conversational style. This is more than just a place to learn about the new flavours of Ragu pasta sauces and apply for coupons: it creates a community of interest around all things Italian including travel, films, language and romance.

Figure 7.1 *Ragu and Mama's Italian Kitchen*

A site's content needs to be structured to reflect what users want to know, not what it is easy for you to provide. Take the example of an online university prospectus. The most obvious navigation model would be to reflect the management structure of the institution. But a survey of sixth-form students identified the top 10 things they wanted from a university prospectus: entry requirements, accommodation information, departmental/course details, general environment of college, details about college social life, course costs, contact names for enquiries, details of local area and nightlife, student services and maps. The site structure should take this into consideration and make sure that key information is readily available, not buried in the detail of each faculty.

Navigation may have to take into account a number of different audiences, and no system is going to suit everybody. Search engines, site maps and indexes help to support whatever structure is used so that even fairly obscure information can be located quickly and easily.

Navigation is commonly facilitated by a navigation bar, introduced on the home page and repeated on every subsequent page. An example from Tide is shown in Figure 7.2. This helps visitors to move from one part of the site to another without the need to return each time to the home page.

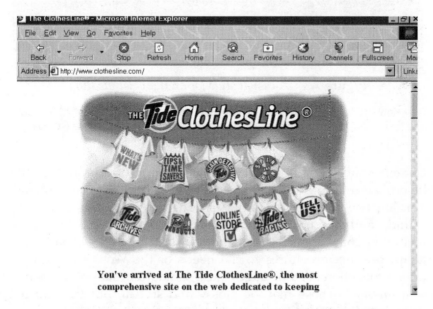

Figure 7.2 *Tide's clothesline acts as a navigation bar*

Tone

The Internet tends to be very informal and laid back in style. The language adopted is spoken English (or whatever language) rather than the formal language of written prose. For example, the original Coca-Cola site (launched in 1995) opened on a chatty note, not just in the words but also in the script they are written in; see Figure 7.3.

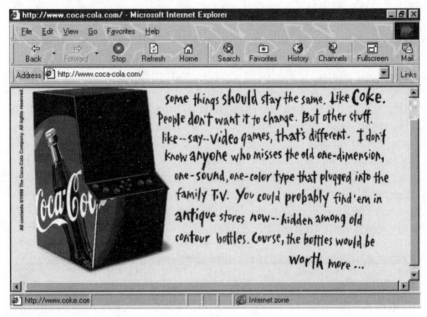

Figure 7.3 *A casual style for an informal medium*

Content that depends heavily on information or editorial should be broken into bite-size chunks or it can become difficult to read. Turning company prose into Web language is not as easy as it sounds, and may need the help of a professional. Many Web sites, including some hi-tech companies, fall into the trap of failing to adapt product brochures to the needs of the Web. They simply offer a collection of static pages like a standard brochure (known as *brochureware*). These may be glossy and stylish, but they do not fully exploit the medium.

Interactivity

As previously discussed, interactivity is the key benefit of the Web, offering visitors the alluring possibilities of participation and instant gratification.

Web users are a new and demanding audience. They have come to expect interactive services such as free information, customization, transaction facilities and chat on the Web. If they come to a site and find nothing of this nature, there is a risk they will be disappointed. They may not actually want to make use of that interactive offer straight away, but they expect it at least to be available.

This may seem obvious, but evidence suggests that companies have not yet learnt to respond to these expectations:

> We found that the vast majority of those organizations surveyed were not engaging in any form of interactive marketing. Their Web sites were merely operating at the most basic level, providing passive information.
>
> Almost half of the Web sites we visited did not request any personal details from visitors. Of those that did, only a tenth asked for anything more meaningful than name and phone number.
>
> It seems that most UK organizations have failed to grasp the basic elements of salesmanship – that is talking to and, more importantly, listening to customers. (1998 study of Times 500 companies by the Cambridge Technology Group.)

PROGRAMMING

Sites that include a dynamic or interactive element, multimedia presentation or database, require programming. Note that such features have a major influence on download time, which in a student survey was cited as the second most important feature of a Web site, after content.

Plug-ins such as Shockwave, Flash, RealMediaPlayer and Director are used to enable the Web browser to execute animation, video and audio files. Microsoft's ActiveX creates active content. *Java* and C++ are advanced programming languages, and *Java applets* are frequently used to add multimedia effects and interactivity to Web pages such as background music, real-time video displays, animations, calculators and interactive games. It is programmes such as these that make the Web truly interactive. They are behind moving images and animations, chat rooms, real-time data feeds, calculations and 'streamed' video and audio (ie, sent in a continuous uninterrupted stream in real time).

If additional software such as a plug-in is needed to access an area of the Web site, it is possible to include on the site a mechanism for automatic download of that software. For example, if a site requires Shockwave player to be installed on the browser so that animated sequences can be shown on screen, include a hyperlink to take the user straight to the Macromedia Web site where download instructions are given.

Technical aspects of a site should be designed with the target user in mind. Multimedia presentations require a lot of bandwidth and may take a long time to download. If users are required to spend time and effort downloading features or applets and extra software such as plug-ins, the information and entertainment value these offer must be worth the waiting time and inconvenience. An estimate of likely download times at different modem speeds is useful, so that visitors can make up their own mind if it is worth waiting for.

When designing a Web site, it is important to pay attention to the speed of users' connections to the Internet and the type of Web browser they are using. Not everybody has cutting-edge machines with the latest browsers and plug-ins. Even students with unlimited free access to the Internet from college computers are not all using the latest spec or running the latest software, nor are they at liberty to install software and plug-ins. 'Mouse Potatoes' (see Forrester Technographic's segmentation model) and teens have the time and patience for downloading sophisticated software, but may be accessing the Web from a second-hand PC with a 14.4kbps modem running on an old version of a browser. Business-to-business sites can use more innovative technology because often the PCs, browsers and servers they use to access the Web have greater technological capacity.

In order to make information accessible to as wide an audience as possible, it is a good idea to provide static *HTML* alternatives to bandwidth-heavy multimedia areas, and consider carefully the impact on accessibility of adding the latest technology to a Web site.

It is important to check that a site works on both of the main Web browsers, Internet Explorer and Netscape Navigator. They operate in slightly different ways, and a page that works well on one may not work at all on the other. Site validators such as Site Inspector (www.siteinspector.com) can check pages for browser compatibility.

HOSTING A WEB SITE

Launching a Web site into cyberspace requires a line connection to the Internet and a *Web server*. The Web server is a computer that is permanently connected to the Internet and deals with requests for Web pages. Setting up a Web server is expensive, as it requires a dedicated computer, high bandwidth connection to the Internet, software, and a Webmaster.

Hosting companies such as ISPs can provide this service more cheaply. They will usually provide the hardware, software and Internet connectivity in return for a monthly fee. The fee will depend on the functionality of the site, and again interactivity, database technology and e-commerce all cost more than static pages. If the Web site is very complex, check that the hosting company can handle your needs.

MAXIMIZING TRAFFIC

Just because a Web site exists does not mean that consumers will visit it. Even if your Web site offers something consumers want, they have to learn about it and find their way to it. A Web site can be promoted in a number of ways, discussed below.

Register with search engines

There are three ways to find an item on the Web: by directly typing a Web address, by following a link from another page or by using one of a number of Web search engines. Reports suggest that over 70 per cent of visits are likely to come from search engines. It is important for a Web site to be indexed and cross-referenced in such a way that it is flagged up by the major search engines used by potential customers.

Include the Web address in offline advertising and promotions

Put the URL (*Uniform Resource Locator*) in traditional print and TV advertisements as well as brand brochures, mailings and other promotional materials. Find innovative ways to make your online brand stand out from the crowd and build brand awareness. Big-Star, an online entertainment store, has plastered its name on the side of 203 trucks in New York, Los Angeles, San Francisco and Dallas, creating the impression that it owns the trucks across the country and is much bigger than it really is.

Advertise the Web site online

The problem with offline advertising is that when people see a URL for a site on a TV advertisement, poster or magazine, they have to remember it when they next access the Web. Remembering URLs can be a problem, particularly as many 'dot com' companies have similar names. For example, Pets.com, Petopia.com, PetSmart.com and Petstore.com are just four of the seven online pet stores.

Online advertising on content sites that attract the target audience has the advantage of immediacy, as a click of the mouse on a hyperlink is enough to transport the visitor to the Web site.

Generate press attention through PR briefings

There has been an explosion of coverage about information technology over the past few years, and every major print and television news outlet has at least one cyberspace beat reporter. Ask your agency to prepare a case study explaining the background, objectives and development of your brand Web site for circulation to relevant industry and marketing publications. Seek out opportunities to talk to the media through press releases and interviews. If you can create a buzz and excitement around your site, people will visit to see what the fuss is about (see 'viral marketing' in Chapter 9).

Trade hyperlinks with other interesting or associated sites on the Web

Identify sites that target a market similar to your own and whose visitors are likely to be interested in your product or service.

Sometimes, a link can be created free of charge and with nothing in return: if someone really likes a Web site, they may provide a hyperlink with their own site just for fun.

It is prudent to check out hyperlinks to avoid surprises. For example, a highly reputable German ice cream site unwittingly provided a link into Parrotthead Madness Boat Drink Mixer page whose disclaimer reads:

> This shit can kill you! It can make you have babies with two heads....
> If you pass out from drinking this stuff don't pass out face up, you
> might choke on your own puke or, worse yet, someone else's puke....
> Do not put body parts in the blender either. It hurts like hell and the
> thrill wears off way too quick....

Provide content to third parties

If you are lucky enough to have content that portal sites feel is useful to their user base, they may ask you to become a content provider. This will help drive traffic to your site.

Send targeted e-mails

Once a site visitor has registered their e-mail address (for a competition, prize draw, etc), send follow-up e-mails to inform that person of site updates and new promotions to encourage repeat visits. For example, the Mum Online site sends an e-mail to all unsuccessful participants of the monthly prize draw to encourage them to enter the next competition. Potential new visitors can also be targeted from mailing lists.

IN-HOUSE OR OUTSOURCED?

A simple Web site with static pages can be developed in-house. Thanks to new software, it is possible to create HTML documents without any knowledge of programming. 'Web authoring' software packages are available that convert electronic copy (for example in Word) into HTML. Graphic design can be accomplished with the help of appropriate graphics software such as Photoshop or FrontPage. These provide wizards and templates to guide design, and the ability to include clip art and photographs.

There are plenty of sites offering a step-by-step guide to creating your own Web site. For example, the Microsoft small business site (www.microsoft.com/smallbiz) introduces users to the process and the tools available (Microsoft software packages) and Whatis.com (www.whatis.com) has information and advice on every step from a range of contributors.

A company with programming talent available internally may also be able to cope with developing sites containing interactive elements. However, there are many Web agencies and consultancies about who are ready to take on these tasks for you.

FUNDING

Unlike traditional media such as TV, where production costs are low relative to the money spent on media placement, the main cost of a Web site lies in production. The cost of placing a site in cyberspace is minimal – hence advertising agencies' reluctance to accept remuneration based on media spend! But if a Web site needs to advertise its presence on other parts of the Web in order to attract visitors, it will incur additional media placement costs.

In the creative development stage, typical expenses include:

▨ concept/idea generation;
▨ overall design style;
▨ structure/site map;
▨ page layouts;
▨ icon design;
▨ agency fees.

Publishing a Web site using static pages may be done very cheaply. Interactive elements add to the costs as they require more programming:

▨ compression of images;
▨ animation of sequences;
▨ applications to view live camera, download video/sound clips, etc.

Customizing a site for relationship marketing, data capture or e-commerce transactions adds significantly to the cost, as database technology is expensive.

Maintaining a good Web site requires resources on an ongoing basis. Content needs to be updated regularly – not just once a year. Technology upgrades need to be installed. Expenses may include:

■ licensed or purchased content agreements;
■ updates;
■ competitions, promotions, etc;
■ links to new sites;
■ running costs of chat lines, e-mail, online transactions;
■ Webmaster/mistress's salary.

And last but not least, the costs of hosting a site and attracting visitors:

■ monthly fee or the cost of a server;
■ creating online advertising and buying space.

It is not possible to give clear guidelines on the cost of setting up a Web site, as it can vary significantly from a simple collection of brand pages to a complex database-driven transaction site. Fortune 500 companies are reported to have spent US $800,000 to US $1.5 million to develop their Web sites and related software. But once a site exists and an audience has been attracted, the variable cost of each additional interaction is relatively low.

Where a company has several different operations or brands, costs can be kept down by avoiding duplication. Rather than set up a separate site for each country, international brands can develop one mega site where all material is shared. This may not be practicable where transactions are involved or the brand has local differences; however, where possible it makes sense to share the cost of designing sophisticated interactive Web material.

Once the real costs and resources required to create and maintain a destination Web site have been fully assessed, the expense may prove difficult to justify on a strictly commercial basis. The Web is still a niche rather than mass medium and the volume of traffic passing through the Web site may be small. However, companies recognizing the need to conduct basic marketing research in this area often treat investment in a Web site as part of a strategic learning process. Some businesses are gaining experience of online retailing now in order to be prepared for the arrival of interactive TV and a whole new range of electronic services.

CHECKLIST

Like any other media project, creating a Web site requires a clear brief against which creative work can be developed and assessed. The brief should include:

■ details of the target audience;
■ the user benefit;
■ campaign objectives;
■ a budget;
■ a time plan.

Evaluate work against these criteria: try to avoid getting carried away with technology if it fails to deliver against your requirements. There are plenty of fascinating Web sites that have no commercial value for their owners.

Chapter glossary

Brochureware A term used to describe Web sites that are little more than online product brochures, ie have few or no interactive elements.
Content The ideas, concepts and formats that attract people to a Web site.
Host A computer with full Internet access.
HTML, Hypertext Mark-up Language A set of instructions within a document that specify how it will appear on your computer screen when you view it on the World Wide Web or offline on your computer. HTML can also include references to still images, video and audio, as well as hyperlinks that enable users to jump between Web pages or sites by clicking on underlined text, highlighted images or icons.

Java A programming language. The most widespread use of Java is in programming small applications, or 'applets', for the World Wide Web. **Java applets** are used to add multimedia effects and interactivity to Web pages, such as background music, real-time video displays, animations, calculators and interactive games. They may be activated automatically when a user views a page, or require some action on the part of the user, such as clicking on an icon in the Web page.

Plug-in A small piece of software that adds extra features to the browser making the Web more interactive. Commonly used to display multimedia presentations in the main window, or access real-time data.

URL, Uniform Resource Locator The unique address of a Web site, consisting of the protocol, server or domain, and then a path and file name for individual pages.

Web server A computer or programme permanently connected to the Internet, running special software that responds to commands from a client.

8

Selling Online

Online retailing today may be tiny, but it is growing fast. Improved security and the realization that good deals and convenient services are available on the Web are increasing consumer confidence.

ELECTRONIC RETAILING

Electronic commerce will eventually affect most of our daily transactions – from the way phone bills are paid and banking is done to booking holidays and buying books. Analysts estimate that Western Europe's e-commerce business will have been worth £11.8 billion in 1999, and that within three years that figure could reach £139 billion. But it is in retailing that the signs of change are first making themselves felt.

Initial predictions were cautious when it came to electronic retailing, also known as *e-tailing*. It was anticipated that security issues would inhibit consumers from giving credit card details and placing orders over the Web, and that in many categories people would be reluctant to purchase without seeing, touching or trying the product first.

But the growth of online shopping has outstripped expectations as consumers find that the benefits of shopping around for low cost and added convenience outweigh the disadvantages. The most popular electronic retail categories, according to a 1999

BMRB International Internet Monitor survey, are books, CDs, computer software, clothes and computer hardware. These are followed by travel accommodation, tickets for events, holidays and airline tickets.

Suddenly retailers are realizing that this is a growing market and they have to be there. In the US, most of the large traditional retailers – including Wal-Mart stores, the world's biggest retailer – already have online stores, but so far they account for an insignificant proportion of sales. Boston Consulting estimated revenue for Internet retailing at US $13 billion for 1998, a mere 0.5 per cent of US retail sales. However, growth is accelerating fast, and Verdict Research predicts online spending in the US will increase by more than 1100 per cent between 1999 and 2004, from US $943 million to US $12 billion. Investment bank Goldman Sachs predicts that 15–20 per cent of the global retail market could eventually be captured by the Internet as more and more shoppers move online.

It is unlikely that online shopping will ever replace 'bricks and mortar' retailing, and many high-street retailers view it as just another channel to get their brand and products to customers. But online shopping will undoubtedly have a significant influence on the way in which retailing develops in the future. People will still go shopping in stores, often for social or for entertainment reasons, but the focus of these trips will change. In response to this change in the nature of shopping, offline retailers need to make the in-store shopping experience more fun and less of a chore.

For example, the advertising campaign for the new Bluewater retail complex in Kent uses the strapline: 'It is as far from being a shopping centre as it is possible to be.' Shopping has a social side that the Internet cannot replicate, and can be seen as a leisure activity. Bluewater aims to create an 'experience' more along the lines of a day out at Disney than a shopping trip. The focus is on increasing spend per head by extending people's stay. In addition to the 320 shops, the park features boating lakes, food courts, entertainment areas, and statues to make it easier to recognize meeting points for families, especially children.

As shopping for basic packaged groceries is increasingly conducted from home, shoppers will have more time to spend on selecting fresh produce and to top-up with non-essential goods and less traditional grocery items during their visits to a store.

Tesco's 'Extra' stores recognize this trend and try to recreate the atmosphere of the high street in a one-stop superstore. The first Tesco Extra was opened at Pitsea in Essex in June 1997 and a second is planned for Peterborough. The Pitsea Tesco Extra offers not only a wide range of food, household goods and clothes, but also a food court for in-store and take-away diners, a flower shop, a print and paper department, a Kids' Club (crèche), a Cookshop, Mother and Baby World, and an in-store theatre. The extra space in the 100,000 square foot store means that Tesco can offer special events, including food sampling and celebrity guest appearances.

A SHOPPER'S HEAVEN

For consumers, online shopping holds out the promise of endless choice, good value and convenience.

> All the goods for sale in the world will be available for you to examine, compare and, often, customize. When you want to buy something you'll be able to tell the computer to find it for you at the best price offered by any acceptable source. Servers distributed worldwide will accept bids, resolve offers into completed transactions, control authentication and security, and handle all other aspects of the marketplace, including the transfer of funds. It will be a shopper's heaven. (Bill Gates)

But a shopper's heaven is potentially a supplier's hell. The scenario depicted holds both opportunities and threats.

Consumer acceptance of online sales gives suppliers the opportunity to increase revenues. It provides access to new markets and to customers who might not otherwise have bought their product or service. It opens up a global marketplace, 24-hour trading and the possibility of lowering sales and customer service costs.

Businesses that need to respond quickly to market changes can introduce simple price changes, short-term promotions and market trials of new products easily. Mail-order and phone-based operations find migration to the Internet relatively straightforward.

For example, traditional catalogue shopping has always appealed to consumer groups such as busy women with small children who prefer the convenience it offers. Specialist online mail order catalogues such as Freemans (www.freemans.co.uk), Racing Green (www.racinggreen.co.uk), Hawkshead (www. hawkshead.co.uk) and LandsEnd (www.landsend.com) have launched Web shopping sites. These are now being joined by Internet start-up companies such as Easyshop (www. easyshop.co.uk) and Boo (www.boo.com).

Low-cost Web operators will increasingly undercut pricing, starting with premium priced market sectors where the value to weight ratio does not make the cost of distribution prohibitive. For example, The Fragrance Counter (www. FragranceCounter.com) is a leading online retailer of designer fragrances for men and women, offering over 1200 brand name items. Through its sister site, The Cosmetics Counter (www.cosmeticscounter.com) consumers can purchase a selection of beauty products. Both services offer free shipping in the US, money-back guarantee, and free gift-wrap.

Companies doing business internationally sometimes maintain different retail prices in different markets, and online sales make these differences transparent and difficult to maintain. Pricing levels are quite commonly higher in Europe than in the USA. This may be justified by local cost structures, delivery costs, or may be opportunistic. Whatever the reason, the only way a company selling from a Web site can protect its pricing structure is by refusing to deliver outside a given territory.

Grey imports may become a problem where a distributor in a low-priced country sells to another company in a higher-priced country. The Internet enables US online mail order retailers to sell direct to European consumers, thus arbitraging the price difference between the markets. This is already an issue in the book trade, where publishers buying UK rights are discovering to their horror that British customers can have books shipped from the US and still save money.

COMPARISON SHOPPING

Bill Gates' vision of the Web as a nirvana of frictionless capitalism where middlemen are obsolete, mark-ups pared to the bone and consumers rule, relies on the development of intelligent agents known as shopping robots, or *shopbots* or bots. These search the Internet for the best prices or shortest delivery times and, with the help of a shopbot, a shopper could in theory eventually find the cheapest price for everything, from books to flowers to spark plugs.

For example, BargainFinder, the original shopbot developed by Anderson Consulting, allows consumers to search half a dozen online music stores and returns with a list of titles arranged by price. Other services like Yahoo's Shopguide, Snap's DealFinder or Viaweb's Shopfind cover a wide spectrum of products, from sporting goods and flowers to computers and peripherals.

In reality, bots are only as good as the information they collect, and there are plenty of ways for uncooperative Web stores to thwart and confuse digital comparison shoppers. Some Web sites block bots, refusing to answer requests for Web pages that come from known bot sites. Alternatively they can confuse the robots by changing the Web site's format or appearance so the bot doesn't know where to look for pricing information, or lower a product's base price, and raise hidden costs such as shipping and handling.

HOME SHOPPING MODELS

According to a 1999 survey by Verdict retail research consultants, 43 per cent of Britain's top 100 retailers have Web sites. But they have been more cautious about setting up online shopping services. Only 14 per cent of UK retailing sites allow transactions, with retailers such as Dixons, WH Smith and Tesco leading the way.

For example, the grocery retailers were quick to establish Web sites, but not necessarily for home shopping. The Asda site (www.asda.co.uk) mixes product information with competitions, and the Safeway Web site (www.safeway.co.uk) is used for graduate recruitment.

The two key components to home shopping formats are:

1. The 'front-end' to the consumer, including ordering via the Internet, catalogues, phone and 'fax back' forms. These ordering interfaces are very much in their infancy, but

technologies exist that are gradually providing easier and more secure ordering services over the Internet.
2. Collection and delivery. Shopping may be delivered to a location of the customer's choice, including home or office, or collected ready-packed from the store. Local train stations and stores are also being considered as alternatives to doorstep delivery so that customers do not have to wait at home for deliveries.

These components can be combined in different ways, as shown by different grocery models. Wal-Mart (www.walmart.com) and US Internet-based NetGrocer (www.netgrocer.com) offer electronic ordering but franchise collection and delivery to third parties (UPS and Federal Express). The Waitrose grocery chain has bypassed the difficulties of delivering to people at home with its Waitrose@Work scheme, and Sainsbury's is testing its Orderline service (www.sainsburys.co.uk) offering a choice of home delivery or collection from store. Peapod in the US (www.peapod.com) and Tesco (www.tesco.co.uk) offer a full service that is branded with their name from order to delivery, and use their own staff throughout. Tesco's extended trial of Tesco Direct (see Figure 8.1) in test areas allows shoppers to browse for purchases either online or on a CD. Orders can be placed and paid for online, and are delivered by Tesco-owned refrigerated vans at specified times for a £5 delivery charge.

THE IMPLICATIONS OF HOME SHOPPING

Home shopping may still be small in volume, but its impact on packaged goods retailing is potentially significant.

Control of the medium means control of the consumer

There was a transfer of power to retailers when retailers' ability to influence shoppers in store began to overshadow the manufacturer's ability to influence consumers in their homes through mass advertising. Eighty per cent of purchase decisions are made in store according to Popai, the point of purchase trade body.

Figure 8.1 *Link to Tesco Direct from the UK Web site*

Brand manufacturers fear that the growth in online retailing opens the door for growth of own-label goods. A retailer who interacts with the shoppers over the phone or the Internet, and delivers goods to their doorstep, may be able to develop a strong relationship with them and influence purchase choice. For example, Tesco could alert the Internet shopper to the savings to be made by switching from a branded product to the own-label equivalent, and offer coupons or free samples targeted directly at brand shoppers.

Some see this as a nail in the coffin of brands, but other brand owners are working in partnership with the retailers. They see an opportunity to use the interactive store environment to attract new and different customers for their brand, increase loyalty through the use of added value information (recipes, magazines, tips, promotions, etc) and stimulate impulse buying. For example, they may offer personalized and cross-category promotions to shoppers, influence the way in which the brand is shown on the 'virtual shelf', or become the category expert by offering advice and services direct to the consumer at the point of purchase. A special loyalty discount can be offered as an incentive for a consumer to place a brand on auto-replenish. Interactive TV may eventually allow consumers to react to a TV commercial directly through a link to further information or by making a purchase.

For example, multinational brand owners are working with Dutch retailer Albert Heijn to learn how to communicate with consumers in an interactive store environment. Unilever has also struck a deal with US NetGrocer, giving it exclusive sponsorship of certain product categories on-site, with sole rights to advertising, marketing and research within them.

Other packaged goods companies are beginning to experiment with their own home shopping services. Nestlé is pioneering an online shopping service giving Swiss consumers the opportunity to order a range of Nestlé foods and confectionery for delivery by the Swiss postal services (www.le-shop.ch), and Avon products can be purchased online (www.avon.com).

The balance of power

But the trend towards home shopping does not necessarily benefit superstores, for a number of reasons:

- Home shopping encourages customers to stay away from superstores, and this migration of business will start to have a negative effect on their profitability. Superstores have been able to offer both lower prices due to economies of scale, and greater convenience in the form of car parks, a broader selection of products, etc. As business flows away from the superstores, their advantages of scale diminish and power over manufacturers will fade.
- Superstores have a real problem with order fulfilment. Instead of the customer turning up at a shop, selecting the products, packing them and then taking them home, retailers have to do it all, pay for it and give a low price. In the case of Tesco and Sainsbury's, an employee strolls around the store picking items off the shelf that have been placed there by another employee. The retailer also has to spend heavily on advertising to attract shoppers. This is not a very profitable model.
- Setting up a home shopping service demands different skills from traditional retailing. Conventional retailing revolves

around property, the in-store environment and merchandising: the success of electronic retailing depends on time (order times, lead times, delivery times) and the interface (such as the phone or Web site).

SETTING UP A TRANSACTION SITE

Setting up a full online sales operation requires the following components:

■ The shop front. A catalogue or virtual store that enables the customer to view the range of products available. Choices are most commonly made by clicking on a shopping trolley icon and dragging the item into the trolley. A search facility may also be included.
■ Ordering facility. Purchase orders can be taken from a Web site in several different ways. Customers can print out an order form to send or fax, send an e-mail or fill in an online order form.
■ System for secure transactions. Payment can be made by traditional methods such as credit card over the phone, but increasingly electronic payment methods are used. Credit card transactions over the Web need to be protected by security systems to prevent hackers from intercepting them.

An important issue for companies setting up online ordering facilities and electronic payments is how these integrate with existing systems such as order processing and stock control.

Software products are available that provide the whole range of services. These include displaying product details held in a separate database, searching for products, filling an electronic shopping basket with purchases, customer identification, online order and payment processing, automated tax and shipping calculations, online order tracking and customer service. For example, Intershop Communications develop and distribute e-commerce software (www.intershop.co.uk).

Some companies now offer complete e-commerce solutions for small to medium size businesses. OpenMarket (www.openmarket.com) has a range of products for electronic business transactions, and provides details of resellers who can provide not just the package but also the expertise to install and implement the package. See also IBM's NetCommerce (www.uk.ibm.com).

ISPs offer hosting and implementation services for electronic commerce sites. For example, ISP Demon offers its subscribers access to a suite of user-friendly management tools which enable merchants to build their own store from an easy-to-use shop generation wizard, and access a secure back office server and transaction processing mechanism. Merchants then need to set up a merchant account with a bank or banking bureau. Free.com.net's eCommerce Package (www.freecom.net) aims to deliver a one-stop service for small businesses to create, run and manage a shop on the Internet, using Intershop software hosted on Hewlett Packard Netservers.

PAYMENT AND SECURITY

Consumer confidence that personal data and credit card information can't be intercepted and decoded is vital for the development of e-commerce. Three basic areas of security need to be considered by a business accepting credit cards from customers over the Internet:

1. Getting the customer's credit card data to the Web site in an acceptably secure manner.
2. Protecting the credit card information from theft.
3. Passing credit card data to the processor in a secure manner.

The key to secure commercial transactions is *encryption*, the process of encoding information to keep it private. Encryption works by substituting different characters for the actual characters and then reversing the process at the end.

Secure Sockets Layer (SSL) is a standard that encrypts data between a Web browser and a Web server. Most types of browsers are SSL-capable, so the cardholder just needs to look for the closed lock or key symbol on the bottom left corner of their browser software. This means that they are on a secure page that has established an SSL 'channel', so their data will be encrypted as it is transported to the secure server.

Any merchant wanting to set up online sales will need to find a supplier with experience of setting up reliable systems for credit card transactions and a system that integrates with the company's existing operations. This is particularly important if orders might start pouring in from around the world, raising questions about currency, customs and shipping.

Despite assurances that systems already in use are practically invulnerable to hackers' assaults, some potential customers may still lack confidence in parting with credit card details over the Internet. To counter this problem, many Web-based shopping services including Virgin (www.virgin.net/shopping) have launched their own 'safe shopping guarantees' with an assurance that if subscribers' cards are used fraudulently and they are penalized for payments imposed by the card issuers (typically £50), they will refund the difference.

CODE OF PRACTICE

Consumer confidence can be undermined not only by security worries but also by hidden charges, non-delivery or dissatisfaction with the goods delivered.

During Christmas 1999, many shoppers were taken by surprise when they received a bill from Customs and Excise for non-European Union goods ordered via the Internet. Some of these extra charges cancelled out the discounts that online retailers claimed to offer. The Government proposes to make it illegal for a UK Web site not to quote prices inclusive of VAT and all customs duties before consumers agree to buy.

In the UK, the Consumers' Association has launched the Which? Web Trader Scheme designed to address such problems. Its Code of Practice covers pricing, payment, delivery, security, advertising, promotions, refunds, complaints, privacy and dispute resolution issues. Web traders who wish to bear the Which? Web Trader logo must agree to meet and abide by this Code of Practice. Complaints from consumers are investigated, leading to possible withdrawal of permission for the trader to display the logo. Full details are available at Which?Online (www.which.net/webtrader).

CHECKLIST

Setting up and administering a full e-commerce site requires technical support and integration with existing systems. It is also important to consider the logistics of fulfilling orders. Can it be shipped economically or delivered digitally? Manufacturers who cannot compete with online retailers of their product may have to find a way to co-operate with them in the online environment rather than set up in competition.

▦ Determine who is going to provide support for each stage of the selling process: promoting, ordering and secure payment.
▦ Consider using the help of third parties.
▦ *Virtual malls* may provide access to shopping trolley software and a central system for transactions in return for a fee, rent or commission on sales. Virtual malls may also be able to attract a higher level of traffic than the independent trader.
▦ Some online retailers offer 'partnering deals'. The retailer handles order processing and delivery, and the partner receives a percentage of profits on products or services sold.

Chapter glossary

E-tailing   Online retailing.
Encryption   The process of making data secure from unauthorized access on the Internet by substituting different characters for the actual characters. The code is then deciphered by the authorized recipient or processor.
Shopbot   Short for shopping robot, a type of intelligent agent. A software tool for digging through data: users give a shopbot directions on what they want to buy and it comes back with details such as prices and availability.
SSL, Secure Sockets Layer   is a protocol for establishing a secure communications channel to prevent the interception of critical information such as credit card numbers. Used to enable secure electronic financial transactions (see *SET*, below) on the Web.
SET   Secure Electronic Transactions specification encrypts data between a Web browser and a Web server, giving online buyers reassurance that their credit card details are safe.

Virtual mall   A collection of transaction sites, often centred round online communities such as AOL. A merchant prepared to pay a fee, rent or commission on sales can access shopping trolley software and use the mall's central system for transactions.

9

Advertising on the Web

The World Wide Web opens up new communication possibilities for personalized messages to be delivered to targeted individuals. Web users are accustomed to being in control of the material they seek and receive on the Internet, but new technologies are being developed that enable advertisers to seek out their target market and 'push' messages at them.

BACKGROUND

The scientists and academics who started the Internet saw no need for advertising support and so gave little thought to the form advertisements might take. This is unlike television and radio, which in many countries evolved hand-in-hand with advertising as a form of mass-market entertainment. Right from the start commercial TV programmes were interspersed with 30- or 60-second slots giving advertisers the opportunity to deliver attention-grabbing messages to vast audiences.

The first Web advertisements appeared in 1994 in the form of banners. Early banner advertisements tended to be static messages rather like small posters, just as early TV ads were often radio ads with pictures or moving press ads. But advertisers increasingly realized that the medium could be used to greater effect.

FROM BROADCAST TO PERSONALIZATION

. Niall Fitzgerald, chairman of Unilever, warns:

> Digitization, the new technology, the convergence of computing and telecommunications sciences, the plunging unit costs of equipment, rising levels of disposable income and the deregulation of the airwaves all mean that simple, one-way, mass communication has its best and biggest days behind it.

Interactivity potentially shifts control from media producers to consumers. Where traditional media producers would simply broadcast information to the public, Web visitors choose what they want to view, when they want to view it.

The Web opportunity is not so much to broadcast a message to a wide/global audience (the mass media still provide a cost-effective alternative), but to target a specific market or individuals. The interactivity of the Web allows messages to be personalized in a one-to-one communication and for a dialogue – leading hopefully to a relationship – to be established.

THE CONCEPT OF 'PUSH'

It is easy to ignore advertising on the Web. Marketers need to be ingenious, beckoning with freebies, discounts, samples and hard-to-find products and finding ways to *push* their message to their target market.

'Push' in Web terms means the delivery of information to a user without it being prompted or 'pulled'. New push technology increasingly finds ways to distribute messages to a defined audience instead of making them go and get it. This can be done in different ways:

▓ Information can be broadcast to everyone who has access to a particular channel or frequency, or who visits a particular Web site. Just like traditional broadcast media such as the TV or radio, Web technology can send messages that appear on all users' screens whether they ask for them or not.

▓ Personalized information can be triggered by a programmed request from the user's computer. Push channels such as

Pointcast (see pages 122–23) require the user to download a programme and to register a profile of interests, and the programme periodically initiates requests for information against that profile on the user's behalf. Intelligent agents are also part of push technology.

▓ E-mail is a form of push, as it arrives because someone has sent it, without necessarily being requested.

ADVERTISING FORMATS

The various formats are shown in Figure 9.1 and discussed below.

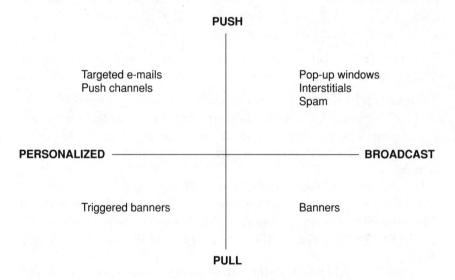

Figure 9.1 *Summary of advertising formats*

Banner advertising

Banners are typically rectangles seen at the top or bottom of Web pages, which viewers are invited to click on with their mouse to get more details. They vary from simple logos to sophisticated graphics with moving images, and can be used to convey a stand-alone brand message, or provide a teaser that attracts the user to click through to the advertiser's site.

A click on a banner advertisement can take the viewer straight to the advertiser's Web site, or initiate a download of software or micro site. Micro sites have the advantage of enabling marketers to interact with their target audience without necessarily taking them away from the environment they had chosen to visit. This type of approach is predicted to grow fast, particularly for relatively low interest products and temporary promotional messages.

The context in which a banner advertisement is placed can be as important as the content. The rate of response can be influenced significantly by the environment in which it is placed. Great content in the wrong place is useless, and banners should be placed in areas that address the same consumer need states as the product or service being promoted. For example, banners advertising Ragu cook-in sauces have received a good response when placed on the 'home arts' pages of community sites.

Triggered banners

Banners can be targeted more closely by triggering them to appear only in response to key words, typically on a search engine. By purchasing key words, it is possible to ensure that a banner is displayed only when the target audience keys in those words for a search.

For example, a user searching for 'allergies' on Yahoo! triggers not only search results (see Figure 9.2a) but also a banner addressing the allergy problem, trying to entice visits by a specific group to the Web site of Claritin allergy medication (see Figure 9.2b).

Technology developments are finding new ways to make clicking on a banner a more interactive experience. For example, consumers who clicked on a Lynx banner placed in media sites were taken into the Lynx Web site, but when they returned to the media site, the original text had been changed or corrupted to incorporate Lynx brand copy. This is known as a parasite banner.

Tips for creative execution

Web advertising is no different from other forms of communication in principle, and traditional communication models such as AIDA can be applied equally well to Web banners as to TV or press advertisements. AIDA is an acronym for Attention, Interest, Desire

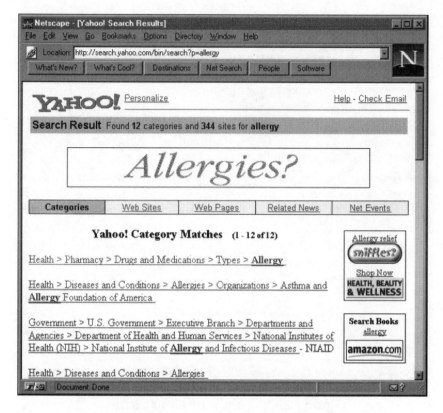

Figure 9.2a *Click on the banner...*

and Action, which summarizes the key steps involved in marketing communications. The model emphasizes that it is important first to grab the attention of your target users, then tell them something that appeals to their self-interest, stimulate desire to try, buy or examine the product, and finally encourage them to take action.

Marketers are increasingly using online advertising as more than a simple attention-grabbing device and exploiting the Web's interactivity to facilitate action. Animation and teaser campaigns encourage visitors not just to look but also to act immediately by clicking through to a Web site, a promotional offer, sampling operation or competition. The most effective banners tend to:

▪ Be brief. The brand message has to compete against content that the visitor was actively looking for and is interested in.

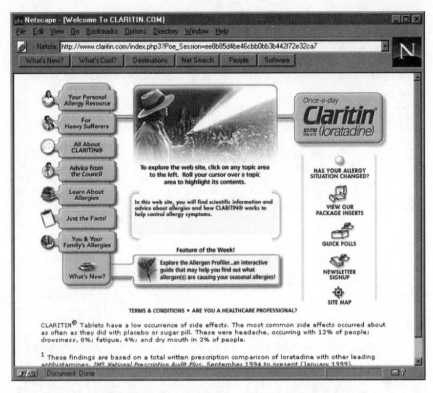

Figure 9.2b *... and learn about Claritin*

■ Be bold. Animated or visually striking banners, or teasers that arouse curiosity, work better than subtle, elegant executions.

■ Keep visuals simple. Resolution is still poor on the Web, and icons read better than complicated images.

■ Give a clear call for action. Tests have shown that using the words 'click here' can increase click rates by as much as 50 per cent.

■ Offer an incentive. Games, quizzes and promotions increase the click rate.

■ Reflect the context. Creative executions should where possible be tailored to the type of site, as relevancy boosts response.

■ Be interactive. Banners that offer interactive experiences and animations outperform static banners.

Banners have the advantage of being very flexible: different messages can be tailored to different targets, and be updated on a daily basis if necessary. But their effectiveness depends on visitors bothering to 'pull' the advertiser's message when they come across it. Banners are often criticized for being small, ineffectual and just too easy to ignore to perform the hard work of building brands and selling products. On average, banner ads achieve a *click through* rate of 2 per cent. In a Jupiter Communications survey, 21 per cent of Internet users polled said they never clicked on ads, while 51 per cent said they clicked only rarely.

Web advertising is becoming increasingly 'in your face'. Rather than waiting for consumers to choose to pull a banner ad, advertisers are using sophisticated technology to push their message in a way that consumers cannot ignore.

Pop-up windows

These separate, self-contained windows can be launched automatically when a user goes to or interacts with a site. They are smaller than the browser screen, which stays visible, and do not transport the user away from the original Web site.

For example, P&G use pop-up windows for Cover Girl, Sunny Delight and Always brands on CondéNet's health and fitness site Phys.com (www.phys.com) (see Figure 9.3) and Pampers and Tide ads pop up while childcare articles are downloaded from ParentTime (www.parenttime.com).

In general, these intrusive ads are more attention-grabbing than banners and increase the click through rate. A pop-up ad for Scope toothpaste in which users could send a postcard 'kiss' to their mothers on Mother's Day achieved a 16 per cent click through rate, versus the industry average for banners of 1–2 per cent. However, they run the risk of alienating people and Web site owners sometimes refuse to accept push advertising for fear of discouraging visitors to their sites.

Interstitial advertisements

Research shows that larger, more complex advertisements provoke a bigger response than do banners. So advertisers are developing formats such as 'interstitials': full screen advertisements that appear while users' computers are downloading pages. Interstitials look and act much like television advertisements.

Figure 9.3 *Pop-up advertising on a magazine site*

But greater sophistication brings other problems. The more complex an advertisement becomes, the longer it takes to download, adding to already frustrating delays. Even in the technologically advanced US, many people's computers lack the capacity to handle so-called rich media ads incorporating sound, animation and 3D. For example, in 1997 P&G came up with an experimental ad for its Bounty kitchen towel in which a virtual 'spill' would spread across the screen before being wiped up by a Bounty paper towel. But the ad found almost no takers because of technological issues such as download times, third-party server integration and browser compatibility.

Push channels

Push channels deliver content to subscribers on topics of their choice and updates that can be downloaded for browsing offline.

For example, the Pointcast Network service (www.pointcast. com) provides registered users with selected topics of interest such as news, stock market information, sports scores and weather from around the world. Information is delivered directly to the desktop, and headline news and advertisements run automatically as a screensaver when a viewer's computer is idle. The service is free to users and funded by advertisers who can target advertising based on user selections.

In 1999, Pointcast was sold, and insiders suggest that the original backers may not even have got back all of their original investment. The service has been combined with eWallet consumer shopping service and renamed EntryPoint.

The ability to interact with users and respond immediately, combined with new push techniques, represents a departure from traditional advertising. And it seems that the more sophisticated Web advertising techniques become, the more intrusive they are likely to be. Some people may not mind this intrusion if it brings them tailor-made and relevant information, and cuts out effort. They may not mind that information is biased in the form of an advertorial if it is delivered personally.

However, it is important not to get so carried away by the technology as to forget that it is the content that is critical, not the vehicle. It can be extremely annoying for anyone visiting a site of genuine interest on the Web to get hi-jacked by a pop-up ad that takes time – and therefore money for users paying for the phone call – to download an unwanted commercial message.

Spam

Solicited e-mailing allows subscribers to dictate the topics on which they wish to receive information and the content is personalized. This is in contrast to unsolicited or junk e-mail, commonly referred to as *spam*. Spam breaks all the rules of direct marketing as there is no targeting and no opportunity to create a meaningful dialogue or relationship with consumers.

For example, Virgin Net is suing one of its former subscribers who used his account to send more than a quarter of a million junk mails to try to sell a database of e-mail addresses. The bulk e-mailing disrupted Virgin Net's computer systems and placed its entire mail service on the dreaded Realtime Blackhole List (RBL), a system which blocks messages from ISPs known to be propagating spam.

There is likely to be a backlash against spam, just as people get fed up with junk mail and faxes. However, the European Union has decided not to ban unsolicited e-mail, with the rider that consumers can sign an 'opt out' register.

MEDIA SPEND

Increasing numbers of large advertisers are integrating online spending into their overall media plans. The 'Advertising Revenue Report' conducted by the New Media Group of PricewaterhouseCoopers measures online advertising revenues. The data is compiled directly from information supplied by companies selling advertising on the Internet, and the data includes online advertising revenues from Web sites, commercial online services, free e-mail providers and all other companies selling online advertising.

In the first six months of 1999, online advertising revenue was more than double that for the same period in 1998. The second quarter saw revenues reach US $934.4 million, and the categories leading online spending were:

consumer-related	29 per cent
computing	22 per cent
financial services	20 per cent
business services	9 per cent
telecom	6 per cent

Banner advertisements are the predominant type of advertising, accounting for 59 per cent, with sponsorships at 28 per cent, inter-stitials 4 per cent, e-mail 1 per cent and other 8 per cent.

The New Media Group chair commented:

> To put this report in perspective we need only go back four short years to 1996, when we reported the full year's ad revenue at US $267 million. The industry has come a long way in that time due in no small part to all segments of the industry realizing that this is the most important part of the equation.

The Advertising Revenue Report is conducted for the Internet Advertising Bureau (see Chapter 11, page 143), and updated numbers are available quarterly from the IAB Web site.

The Web advertising market is expected to reach US $4.4 billion in the year 2000, but to put this into perspective, it still represents a very small proportion of the total ad spend of US $131 billion. P&G spend US $3 billion a year on advertising but was spending only US $3 million a quarter in 1999 on interactive ads, despite its public commitment to the medium.

THE NEXT GENERATION

Many people feel that Internet advertising in its present form is a waste of money and want to change the landscape by more sophisticated means of prompting that all-important interaction. Advertisers are looking for novel ways to take Web advertising forward in the new millennium.

New forms of communication are being developed. In 1998 Unilever forged alliances with Microsoft and AOL to work on building innovative programmes and interactive advertising executions beyond the current banners, which can be 'more of a nuisance and clutter than an attraction'. They are looking at opportunities to extend sponsorship and integrate brand messages with content. Unilever messages might begin to appear on such high interaction areas as message boards, live events, even e-mail.

There is increasing interest in Web marketing circles in *viral marketing*, or *buzz marketing* techniques. These are any marketing techniques that induce Web sites or users to pass on a marketing message to other sites or users, creating a potentially exponential growth in the message's visibility and effect. Sites that answer a specific need and let consumers share the solution may succeed in spreading by word of mouth (or word of mouse!).

For example, ICQ enables PC users to talk to each other in real time over the Internet. But both parties need specific software to do so. Users encourage friends to get the free download so they can join in. The ICQ customer base developed without the ICQ management having to do anything.

Interactive broadcasters are promising their advertising partners a range of digital interactive advertising and e-commerce services. For example, in interactive advertising trials for Microsoft's Web TV, viewers will be invited to access additional promotional information during commercial breaks by clicking on screen icons which will take them to Web addresses specified by advertiser partners, including AA Insurance, Bass, Peugeot, Vauxhall, Orange, Barclaycard, Honda, Tesco and Goldfish.

CHECKLIST

■ Integrate Web advertising with the rest of your media campaign to enhance rather than replace more traditional media.

■ Keep up to date with the latest advertising technology. Change happens fast on the Internet, and by the time this book is published new techniques and thinking will already be available.

■ To keep up to date you can ask your agency to review activities of leading-edge Web advertisers such as Unilever and P&G. It's also a good idea to read the marketing press.

Chapter glossary

Click through   The number of users who click on a banner ad and visit the Web site it is promoting, as opposed to the number of users who simply see the banner advertisement.

Push   Delivering a message to the consumer instead of making him or her go and get it.

Spam   Automated e-mail or junk mail.

Viral marketing   A new Web term used to describe any technique for getting users to spread the word about a Web site or service. When a site provides a solution to a consumer need that gets everybody talking about it, this is also known as **buzz marketing**.

10

The Law and Cyberspace

The Internet community is made up of diverse interests that have yet to reach consensus about how to govern the global network. Industry is under pressure to put together a comprehensive self-regulatory framework. Meanwhile, marketers need to take what steps they can to protect their brands and to stay legal in cyberspace.

LEGISLATION VERSUS SELF-REGULATION

There is no one law that governs the whole of the Internet. Companies wanting to attract customers from different countries face a vast array of different laws and regulations, from copyright and trademarks to advertising standards, competition law and third-party liability.

Many Internet enthusiasts would like to keep government in all its guises – regulation, setting of standards, censorship and taxes – well away. They argue that the medium can be controlled through voluntary self-regulation. David Farber, a founding father of the Internet, says:

> If we blow it, the result will be governance by governments with all the negatives that holds for the future evolution of the Net. I wonder if the Net establishment is indeed willing to be grown up – or will they fight till there is nothing left?

But the commercialization of the Internet has already led some local governments to intervene. The German government in 1997 passed a 300-page Multimedia Law, regulating everything from online identity authorization to obligations of Internet service providers, and Hong Kong has introduced laws governing Internet copyrights.

The development by US and European companies of an industry framework is under discussion in Brussels. This would include taxation and tariffs on goods and services sold over the Internet, intellectual property rights, data protection, encryption, authentication of user identities on the Internet and liability issues concerning the transport of illegal content on the Internet.

WHOSE REGULATIONS?

Anyone who trades or advertises on the Web needs to be aware of the laws in individual countries. However, the first difficulty is determining the place of business for Internet activities: a Web site or advertisement can be downloaded from practically every country in the world. Does a customer downloading a page from the Web constitute a 'virtual visit' by the supplier/advertiser to the customer, or a 'virtual visit' by the customer to the supplier's place of business? The place of business for companies supplying online goods or services might be deemed to be either the company's headquarters or the location of the customer in question.

Problems may arise where an advertisement is banned from being downloadable in one country but is legal in all other countries. Some material will be offensive and against the law in certain states – such as showing a woman's legs, using certain religious symbols or advertising alcohol.

To confuse matters further, there are arguments in some countries about just which existing regulatory authorities should have the right to oversee the Internet. Is it broadcasting, other media or even telecommunications? As a result it is not even clear in many countries which regulator is, or will be, in charge.

Some of the areas covered by existing legislation in the UK are:

▦ Misrepresentation. Information aimed at making a sale must be accurate and comprehensive. If not, it can count as a misrepresentation, which can lead to civil liability for damages.

▧ Gambling. This is regulated by statute, and includes all forms of gambling and lottery. A lottery involves the entrant paying something for a chance to win a prize. This is why many advertisements for competitions say 'no purchase necessary'.

▧ Defamation. It is possible to sue the owner of a Web site or sender of e-mail for defamation.

REGISTERING DOMAIN NAMES

Anyone setting up a Web site needs to secure a Web address or *domain name*, such as www.jobloggs.com.

In 1992 the US government gave Network Solutions Inc a legal monopoly on registering all Web addresses ending in '.com', '.org' and '.net'. Internet addresses were initially assigned on a first-come, first-served basis with priority rights for companies with US federal trademarks. This caused resentment among European firms. The US government stopped funding the pact in 1996, allowing Network Solutions to earn revenue by imposing a registration fee instead. The cooperative agreement expired in September 1998, when competition was introduced into the market for registering World Wide Web addresses.

Between April and October 1999, 87 companies gained accreditation from The Internet Corporation for Assigned Names and Numbers (ICANN), which is responsible for managing the domain name system. This allows them to register domain names ending in .com, .net and .org. The ICANN Web site lists accredited registrars worldwide (www.icann.org). The registry for all domain names ending in .uk is managed by Nominet UK, which provides a search facility (www.nic.uk) for Internet users enabling them to find out whether a domain name is available and, if not, who has registered it.

Small businesses and individuals are pushing for the creation of additional top-level domain names – the suffixes on Internet addresses like .com, .net and .org – as this will increase the odds of obtaining their own preferred addresses. But large trademark holders prefer to limit the number of domain names to reduce the opportunities for others to co-opt their brand names. It is one thing for Coca-Cola (www.coke.com) to make sure no one is trying to do business as www.coke.org, but it would be far harder to police dozens of domains and ferret out, for example, www.coke.web or www.coke.store. (Some firms are rushing to register Internet names in Turkmenistan, just in case a governing body one day decides to make the country's Internet designation '.tm' mean 'trademark' and afford some protection.)

Domain names are still registered on a first-come, first-served basis, and this can cause problems for two companies with the same name. If a company finds out its name has already been registered, there are three things it can do: begin litigation, take another name, or buy back its own name.

Entrepreneurs sometimes known as 'cybersquatters' register many well-known names, hoping to sell them on for large profits. One such firm of dealers registered domain names including Marks & Spencer, Virgin, the Spice Girls, Buckingham Palace, *The Times*, Ladbroke, J Sainsbury and BT with the intention of selling the names back to those companies. However, in a landmark ruling in 1998, the Court of Appeal upheld a previous ruling that to register a distinctive domain name could amount to passing off and trademark infringement. The owners of the registered trademarks were granted an injunction against the dealers. The Lord Justice ruled that, 'The domain names were registered to take advantage of the distinctive character and reputation of the marks. That is unfair and detrimental.'

As the Internet becomes used increasingly as a forum for public opinion and consumer rage, companies are rushing to protect themselves by registering sites with negative variations of their name to stop others getting there first. Chase Manhattan Bank has taken out the rights to 'chasestinks.com' and 'chasesucks.com', but was too late to register 'chase-manhattansucks.com', which belongs to an angry customer complaining that his credit card was wrongly billed for US $650.

Even though Web site owners can be sued for libel, negative Web sites are full of outrageous attacks and, for the time being, are getting away with it. For example, after an argument with store staff resulting in being banned from the store, a Wal-Mart customer launched www.walmartsucks.com and claims to receive 2,000 visits a day. Over 1500 customers have e-mailed him with allegations about rude managers, insects in the aisles, and even with tips on shoplifting. There is a section for disgruntled employees, some of whom are obsessed with accusing supervisors of marital infidelities. Wal-Mart's lawyers threatened the site owner with legal action unless he closed the site within 48 hours. He ignored them and announced his plans to sell anti-Wal-Mart mugs and T-shirts on the site.

TRADEMARKS AND COPYRIGHT

Registering a trademark enables the owner of that mark to stop anyone else using it or anything else confusingly similar. The reason why Marks and Spencer, Virgin and the other major companies were able to stop someone else using their name on the Internet was because it was an infringement of a trademark. The Internet is not restricted to national boundaries, so companies wishing to protect their intangible assets need to consider registering brand trademarks internationally.

Copyright is the right to publish and distribute a literary, dramatic or musical work. The definition of these words has been stretched to include computer programmes (literary work), advertising executions (dramatic work) and TV jingles (musical work), though the work has to be original to be protected by copyright. The law of copyright works in cyberspace just as in other media, but in practice it is difficult to enforce and piracy is a growing problem.

For example, in the music industry, the availability of MP3 compression technology enables material to be downloaded to digital quality. A pirate Web site may make it known that the latest Spice Girls' album will be available to download free between certain hours, attracting a teen audience and enabling it to sell guaranteed tightly targeted advertising. The music industry responds by constantly closing down illegal Web sites.

GUIDELINES FOR STAYING LEGAL

Eventually, an international code on consumer protection may evolve, but in the meantime marketers can follow certain guidelines to minimize the risk of breaking the law and to protect their property:

■ Make sure that the content of your Web site or advertisement is accurate and up to date. In virtually every country it is against the law to make misrepresentations about goods or services. Virgin Atlantic allegedly breached US advertising regulations when it advertised on its Web site a fare between London and Newark, New Jersey, that was not available at the time. Virgin is a UK company but it was fined US $16,000 in the US for breach of US law.

■ Get permission before using anyone else's trademark, music, drawings, designs or software.

■ Draw up a contract with the person commissioned to produce a Web page in which he or she assigns all copyright and waives all moral rights, including the right to be identified as the author of a copyright work. This also stops the designer using the work for a competitor or other third party.

■ Put a copyright and other rights notice on the Web page. If information can be downloaded say what users can use it for – whether just to print it and keep it or whether they can supply it to other people or re-use it in works of their own. Use words like: '© Jdavisplc 1998. All rights reserved. You are licensed to download, store and print from this Web site but not to use our material in any other way nor for any commercial purpose.'

■ Check that Web page advertising does not break any existing distribution agreements or other contracts. For example, you may not have the right to advertise outside an allotted territory. For new contracts, clarify whether Internet advertising is allowed.

■ Avoid using competitors' trademarks in comparative advertisements – ie, those directly comparing products with that of a competitor. Although some countries allow this type of advertising if it is 'honest', many countries ban it. New amendments to an EU law on comparative advertising were agreed towards the end of 1997, but the Web page will be seen all over the world.

■ Design the Web site in such a way that customers have to see any disclaimers, terms of sale or supply on the Web page before placing an order. Make it absolutely clear when, and if, a legal contract is made and reserve the right to reject the order.

▓ Limit the countries to which you sell. For example, use the words, 'We take orders from the EU and USA only' – particularly if the product or service may be illegal in some countries, or someone else owns the supplier's trademark in one state with the effect that sales there would breach trademark laws.

DATA PROTECTION

Information about people's behaviour is key to helping Web marketers decide how best to exploit the Net commercially. The personal data industry is developing tools designed to store, sort and sell the most intimate details of consumers' lifestyle. But advances in database technology pose an ever-growing threat to the privacy of individuals.

Efficiently targeted and customized products and services on the Web can provide benefits for online shoppers, but the idea of being monitored covertly is unattractive. Concern over privacy prevents many consumers from sharing personal information with online marketers, or encourages them to give inaccurate information about themselves. The use of cookies and other technological means to track behaviour is seen as encroaching on the user's right to privacy. Emerging consumer groups such as Junkbusters (www.junkbusters.com) are dedicated to lobbying government and showing users how to 'Master self-defence against privacy-invading marketing' with, for example, detailed information on what cookies do and how to avoid them.

In the UK, information recorded from a visit to a Web site is subject to the Data Protection Act. Companies intending to collect data about visitors to their Web site must register as a data user. A set of guidelines has been published by the Data Protection Registrar (www.dataprotection.gov.uk). The EU Directive on Protection of Personal Data, effective since October 1998, lays down some strict common rules (see www.privacy.org):

▓ Data can only be collected for specified, explicit and legitimate purposes, and held only if it is relevant, accurate and up to date.
▓ The collection of data should be as transparent as possible, giving individuals the option of whether they provide information or not.

■ Individuals are entitled to be informed at least about the identity of the organization intending to process data about them and the main purposes of such processing.

■ Data subjects have the right to access data, to know where the data originated (if available), to have inaccurate data rectified, to have recourse in the event of unlawful processing and the right to withhold permission to use their data. For example, individuals have the right to opt-out free of charge from being sent direct marketing material, without providing any specific reason.

■ Sensitive data such as ethnic or racial origin, political or religious beliefs, trade union membership and data concerning health or sexual life can only be processed with the explicit consent of the individual.

Measures such as these may inhibit the Web's ability to realize its full one-to-one marketing potential, but hopefully will help to ensure the free flow of information services by fostering consumer confidence.

The US industry is making attempts at self-regulation, preferring to have an organization to police its members and deal with consumer complaints. Self-regulation is widely viewed in Europe as the equivalent of leaving the fox guarding the chicken run, and there is much anecdotal evidence to suggest that the industry's record to date is not good:

■ A 1999 Federal Trade Commission survey claimed that 89 per cent of sites targeting children collect personally identifiable data from the children themselves, and less than a quarter asked the children to get parental permission to do so.

■ A man slipped, fell and destroyed his kneecap in a San Diego grocery store. When he sued, the grocery store's lawyers delved into their records, saw the man had a discount card and a taste for alcohol, and used the information to deflect responsibility for the accident.

■ A woman received a threatening letter from a convicted rapist who had somehow got access to a database containing some 900 discrete pieces of personal information about her.

In the US, independent initiatives such as TRUSTe whose 'mission is to build users' trust and confidence in the Internet by promoting the principles of disclosure and informed consent' review and audit their members' privacy policies and award a TRUSTe mark to those that comply with their standards. Businesses are encouraged to publish their privacy policies, as demonstrated by IBM:

> At IBM, we intend to give you as much control as possible over your personal information. In general, you can visit IBM on the Web without telling us who you are or revealing any information about yourself. There are times, however, when we may need information from you, such as your name and address. It is our intent to let you know before we collect personal information from you on the Internet.
>
> If you choose to give us personal information via the Internet that we and our partners may need – to correspond with you, process an order, or provide you with a subscription, for example – it is our intent to let you know how we will use such information. If you tell us that you do not wish to have this information used as a basis for further contact with you, we will respect your wishes. We do keep track of the domains from which people visit us. We analyze this data for trends and statistics, and then we discard it.
>
> There is a technology called 'cookies' which can be used to provide you with tailored information from a Web site. A cookie is an element of data that a Web site can send to your browser, which may then store it on your system. Some IBM pages use cookies so that we can better serve you when you return to our site. You can set your browser to notify you when you receive a cookie, giving you more chance to decide whether to accept it.
>
> IBM is also supporting the development of some technologies that will let you manage and control the release of your personal information wherever you go on the Internet. From time to time we'll be sharing information with you about efforts underway in organizations such as the World Wide Web and TRUSTe.

CHECKLIST

When developing a Web campaign, you should go through the same checks and procedures as for a normal advertising campaign. It is usually the responsibility of the marketing function to get clearance for advertising and promotions from a legal adviser, and this is doubly important when embarking on a new media project. There is a lot of uncertainty, anarchy and piracy on the Internet, but the basic principles of trademark, copyright and data protection still apply.

In addition to the guidelines already given, it makes sense to:

▪ Register your domain name before someone else does. Check availability of domain names either through a registration company such as Register.com (www.register.com) or Net-names (www.netnames.com), or directly with Nominet UK (for .uk domain names only).

▪ Make sure that, if you register a name that is also a trademark, your Web site makes it clear that the name or logo is a trade-mark and that its use is restricted.

▪ Register the trademark in every country from which you are likely to seek customers on the Web.

▪ Decide what brand material you want to copyright, and check that you can prove that it is original. Check who has the copy-right on existing Web material: if the contract that appoints the Web designer does not make it clear, the consultant or agency may retain the copyright by default.

▪ Get permission from the owner of the copyright *before* your Web site or advertisement goes online, if you plan to use an existing design, picture, piece of music or text.

▪ Make sure that you are registered as a data user with the Data Protection Registrar if you intend to collect data about visitors to your Web site.

Chapter glossary

Domain name Every Web site and Internet address is given a name. An e-mail address usually consists of a name followed by '@' and then a location ending in '.com', '.ac', '.edu', '.net' or '.org'. Everything after the '@' is known as the domain name. See also 'URL' in the Glossary at the back of this book.

11

Research and Evaluation

Enthusiasts may hail the Web as the ultimate accountable medium, as it is easy to tell how many 'hits' a Web site receives or how many times a banner ad is seen and downloaded. But online audits are limited in the information they can provide on individual visitors unless the right systems are in place, and the Internet cannot provide a representative sample for quantitative investigations. Measurement standards must be agreed before comparisons of Web efficiency with that of other media can be made.

BACKGROUND

In the commercial world, marketers need to evaluate the effectiveness of their online initiatives and to assess the return on investment. Quantified measures and benchmarks are required to compare results with alternative channels of communication or distribution.

However, the scientists and academics who developed the World Wide Web were mainly interested in the free movement of information. They had no commercial motivation, and did not put in place structures and frameworks for accurate assessment.

Attempts to measure accurately are frustrated by the culture of anonymity and freedom of information that has grown up around the Internet. Trying to get individuals to register their personal profiles and to share information for commercial purposes is not always appreciated. Another factor is the lack of industry standards and benchmarks, which makes comparison with other media difficult as there are many different ways to measure a Web audience.

TARGETING CONSUMERS

Quantified and qualitative surveys can identify the demographic and psychographic profile of general Internet users. ISPs are able to collect limited data on new subscribers to their service. But marketers would ideally like to know much more about exactly who visits which Web sites, and why:

▓ content providers and community sites are keen to monitor the identity, profile and activities of their users so that they can sell a tightly targeted audience to advertisers;
▓ promotional and corporate site owners need to measure visitor profiles to assess relative effectiveness of the Web versus other media;
▓ a business building a customer database for relationship marketing purposes needs information on addresses, phone numbers, e-mail, interests and purchases, category usage, level of consumption, demographic and psychographic data and so on.

Web site owners try to capture user profile information either openly through registration schemes and questionnaires, or anonymously through tracking devices.

Registration

User data can be captured through registration schemes, where site visitors are asked to complete a questionnaire on their first visit, and then enter a password on subsequent visits. In general, consumers are more willing to release information about themselves if they receive a real benefit in return or can win a prize. For example, home delivery of goods, personalized shopping accounts and recommendations. The Ragu site (www.eat.com) sends by post paper discount coupons to users who provide their names and addresses.

Mandatory registration may put people off entering a site, and it is not very accurate as people forget their password and register again, causing duplication. For this reason, some press sites that initially set up questionnaires to capture the profile of all visitors now resign themselves to measuring 'gross heads'. However, the need to show advertisers who is using the sites and sell targeted advertisements has led online press sites such as *The Guardian* (www.guardian.co.uk) to introduce a registration scheme. This may result in fewer visitors, but it is an investment in information that can attract advertising revenues.

Users may be reluctant to identify themselves accurately for a number of different reasons. Sometimes it's from necessity – if a UK citizen wants to register on a US site or access information limited to US citizens, he or she may resort to entering a 'borrowed' zip code. Sometimes it's from whim – many people resent the intrusion of personal questions or are suspicious of how it will be used. And sometimes it's to maintain anonymity – you may have good reason for not wanting to be identified visiting some sites!

Cookies

Cookies have the advantage of requiring no direct input from the user. When a user visits a Web site a cookie or small data file can be sent from that site to the user's Web browser and then stored on his or her hard disk. The cookie can record the user's movements within that site and other information such as his or her e-mail address.

Each time a user visits a Web site, the browser looks on the user's hard disk to see whether a cookie exists for that site. If so, it is sent to the server as part of the request for the Web page, and the server can then interpret the information held in the cookie and return appropriate content. Not only do cookies help to build up a picture of users' behaviour and preferences in Web sites, but they also allow the site owner to personalize a site and customize services accordingly.

Cookies may be linked to marketing databases that control banner adverts for targeted advertising. They can tell companies how visitors spend their time on the Internet, and can keep track of individuals' interests by recording the search words they enter into search engines.

Cookies are limited, however, as they can only identify computers and not necessarily the people who use them. With family use of the same computer it becomes increasingly difficult to identify individuals or track their activities. Nor are cookies 100 per cent reliable for market research or targeted advertising, because users can always delete cookie files or set their browsers to notify them of cookie files and refuse to accept them.

TRAFFIC ANALYSIS

A range of data is collected on the Web server's *access log*. These statistics monitor the number of requests to view the home page, the visitors' domain name (for example, visitors from .edu, .com and .gov sites), the number of requests made for each page, and usage patterns by time of day, day of the week and seasonality. This information is used to analyse Web 'traffic' and a number of different measures are commonly used.

Hits record the number of times items or files are downloaded. This is a very broad and fallible unit, as one page may be made up of a number of different files. A Web site wanting to double its traffic overnight need only split the images on its home page into two files. This is going out of fashion as a measurement tool.

Page impressions and page views record the number of times a Web page has been downloaded. There are different ways of reporting traffic: if a Web site has three advertising banners on a certain page, the site could report 300 impressions (100 for each advertisement), though the page was only viewed 100 times. There is also controversy over whether to count pages that have been distributed automatically: content that is pushed or generated by intelligent agents and robots is often not viewed, so electronic page impressions cannot be seen to have the same value as regular page impressions.

Click through is the term used for the number of times an advertising banner is not just seen on the host page, but actually downloaded, ie when the user clicks on the banner with his or her mouse.

Visits measure the number of timed visits or sessions on a Web site. If a user remains dormant for a period of time (normally 30 minutes), the next activity by that user is considered a new visit.

Traffic by page records which Web pages are downloaded during a visit.

Repeat visits are measured by the server log, which can track the habits of repeat visitors through cookies and determine the page requests associated with them.

The depth of information that a Web audit can reveal depends on how a site collects its own information. If it requires registration on entry to the site that collects demographic data, then during each visit every hit in the log file is tied to the person registered. Each page impression can be analysed against the registered user's profile.

Without registration details, analysis of Web traffic is limited. It is possible to determine the number of hits, the route users took through the Web pages, the time spent on each page, but not how many of those hits are first-time viewers and how many are repeats. Web logs use *Internet Protocol (IP) addresses* to track traffic, but this does not correlate with individual people because:

▨ *dial-up* users are usually assigned a different IP address each time they connect to their ISP, and the same IP address may be reused by different people;

▨ users of commercial online services (eg AOL, Compuserve) access the Internet through a limited number of Internet 'gateways', each with its own IP address;

▨ different people can use the same computer to visit the same Web site. Corporate users connect through *proxy servers*, each with its own IP address. Community terminals in libraries and cafés allow many people to use the same computer.

This makes it difficult to audit the traffic on a site in a meaningful way, particularly against the objective of repeat business. Moreover, most banner advertising does not ask people to give any indication of who they are, so it is very difficult to tell whether they have visited the site before.

A further complication to data collection is the practice known as *caching*. In order to cut down redundant network traffic and to speed loading, browsers and proxy servers often save copies of frequently requested pages of popular sites. That way, when a page is requested it doesn't have to be downloaded all over again. For measurement purposes this can cause confusion; for example, it is not necessarily possible to tell how many times a banner advertisement has been seen once it has been downloaded.

ADVERTISING COSTS

Not only is it difficult to establish whether a Web site delivers the desired target audience, but the pricing model for advertising is also subject to some debate.

Content providers initially sold advertising space on the basis of page impressions, but advertisers argue that a banner has little effect unless the consumer clicks on it and links to the promotional site. This raises the debate over how the cost per thousand (cpm) for Web advertising should be calculated, for example:

■ by exposure, measured by page impressions;
■ by response, measured by 'click throughs' to the advertiser's site;
■ by action, measured by download, information exchange or a transaction.

Pricing considerations also include elements such as positioning on the content provider's site (location on home page, e-mail screens or chat-room screen) and pop-up or interstitial messages.

INDUSTRY STANDARDS

The largest Web sites turn to third-party research firms for information on the demographics and size of their audience. But even these do not deliver definitive numbers; research methods differ for everything from choosing audience samples to projecting the total number of visitors to a site. There is a need for agreement of industry definitions and standards of measurement.

The frustration felt at the lack of accountability and comparability of this new advertising medium is reflected in industry initiatives to tackle the issues, which are discussed below.

The Internet Advertising Bureau

The Internet Advertising Bureau (IAB) is a voluntary organization involved in evaluating and recommending standards and practices, conducting research into the effectiveness of the online medium and educating the advertising industry about the use of online advertising.

Founded in 1996, it has over 300 active members worldwide, including companies that are actually engaged in sales of Internet advertising. Associate members include companies that support advertising – interactive advertising agencies, measurement companies, research suppliers, technology suppliers, traffic companies and other organizations from related industries. Visit the Web site (www.iab.net) for news and information including latest research reports, articles on topics such as 'What advertising works?', Internet industry organizations and contacts.

The IAB has formed an industry-based working group to address the problem of multiple standards in the industry of Web traffic measurement. This plans to address three major areas:

1. Best practices – intended to 'raise the bar' on the quality of online audience research by establishing voluntary minimums that conform with generally accepted research practices.
2. Education – intended to aid the online advertising and marketing community in comparing the research results available from different measurement companies.
3. Research – intended to explore and explain the differences among the various measurement companies, and to experiment with new ways to generate more accurate audience counts.

P&G Fast Forum

In an unprecedented move, in August 1998 P&G invited dozens of advertisers (including arch-rivals Unilever) to a 'summit' in Cincinnati, to discuss the difficulties confronted by marketers using online media. Topics covered ranged from inconsistent standards of measurement, through incomplete data on effectiveness, to infighting among the advertisers, agencies and media.

As a result, a new industry group including advertisers, agencies and consumers was set up to:

▓ draft standards for measuring on-line audiences (currently each measurer does its own thing, bewildering advertisers);

▓ establish a set of advertising types or BAIUs (Broadly Accepted Interactive Units) that World Wide Web sites will accept (many sites currently won't accept the complex displays big advertisers increasingly prefer for fear of deterring consumers);

▓ develop a way to reconcile contradictory data supplied by various rival on-line research services.

They are also working on hard evidence on Internet performance, building a common lexicon, educating the marketing community at large on the medium and setting standards of privacy protection.

MARKET RESEARCH ON THE WEB

The Web offers potential market research benefits in the form of low cost fieldwork. It is cheap to compile lists of people with Internet addresses, and send out questionnaires by e-mail. This can save significantly on the cost of face-to-face or properly random telephone-based interviews, which is a major part of the cost of conducting quantified research. However, as the chairman of BMRB International warns:

> Using the appropriate technology, conducting online market research can be quite straightforward. But the problem with the Internet continues to be that it cannot deliver a representative sample of any population. And this problem of representation is fundamental to conducting mainstream consumer research on the Internet, in the same way as it was for the telephone 30 years ago.

Esomar, the Europe-wide umbrella group for market research professionals, has developed guidelines for market research on the Internet; these can be found on their Web site (www.esomar.nl/ guidelines/internet_guidelines). Esomar is investigating the methodological problems and professional issues arising from Internet-based research.

Many research companies in the US and UK are looking to compile lists of Internet users identified through traditional research techniques, who can be recruited on to properly selected panels of online consumers. NOP for example conducts regular surveys aimed at establishing the pattern of Internet use in the UK.

The Internet is, however, suitable for testing reaction to a Web site, or testing a Web concept among general users. TV advertising and product design executions on the Web will eventually be able to be researched online, once graphics software and improved bandwidth enable high-resolution graphics to be downloaded to a high quality.

EVALUATION TECHNIQUES

A number of standard research techniques can help marketers to evaluate the efficacy of their Web site in achieving its objectives. For example:

▓ Focus groups, either on or offline, to expose consumers to the site and explore their reactions to navigation, content, impact on brand equity and areas for improvement. Online focus groups can be conducted in chat rooms with a moderator.
▓ A quantified communications check to measure the impact of the Web site in terms of brand image attributes and purchase intentions. Research to test for significant differences between two samples (one of visitors, the other non-visitors) can be conducted in the traditional way offline.
▓ An online survey addressed to Web site visitors asking for feedback on how they found the site, which other sites they have visited, etc. Remember that this will not give you a representative sample, and should only be used for generating ideas.
▓ Analysis of sampling programme results. The number of unique requests for samples, coupons, etc and the conversion rate can be monitored, and the redemption rates and delivery cost compared with traditional methods of sample/coupon distribution (newspapers, in-store, direct mail).

CHECKLIST

Consider the objectives of your Web campaign and decide what measurements are most important before designing your Web site:

▦ If the objective is to generate loyalty, you will want to measure repeat visits to your Web site and build a profile of visitors. A registration scheme is advisable for the collection of meaningful data.

▦ If the objective is to gain awareness and attract the maximum number of visitors, then measuring the number of hits and page impressions may be adequate. Cookies can help to add some extra detail, without deterring visitors from coming to your site.

▦ Use a reputable and well-established company to audit Web traffic data. For example, the Audit Bureau of Circulation has set up an electronic division for this purpose (www.abc.org.uk/electronic). It also monitors other media circulation and viewing figures, so has experience of generating data in a form that can be compared across media.

It is worth visiting the IAB Web site (www.iab.net) periodically for updates on industry discussions, and articles of interest. You may consider joining the organization if you want to participate in the conferences and newsletters.

Chapter glossary

Access log A list of all the requests for individual files that people request from a Web site.

Cache When a user explores the Web, his or her browser keeps track of the pages visited and saves them on the hard disk so they will load faster when the user wants to return to them. This saves time and money because saved pages can be viewed without being connected to the Internet.

Dial-up A telephone connection to the Internet that is established and maintained for a limited duration, unlike a 'dedicated' connection, which is continuous or always 'on'.

Hit   The number of times an item or file is downloaded from a Web page. When a user arrives at a new site and the site appears on the screen, every text and graphics file associated with that page is a hit. A page with five graphics and text would register six hits.

Internet Protocol (IP) address   A unique numeric identification for a specific Web site or Internet address. The Internet does not recognize word addresses, so name servers translate the URL into an IP address in order to locate the computer on which a Web site or domain name lives.

Page impressions   The number of times a Web page has been downloaded.

Proxy server   A server that acts as an intermediary between a workstation and the Internet. Used by companies to ensure security and administrative control, and may also have a caching service.

Visits   The number of timed visits or sessions on a Web site. If a user remains dormant for a period of time (normally 30 minutes), the next activity by that user is considered a new visit.

12

What Next?

Rapid growth in the 1990s has transformed the Internet from a practically unknown tool for 'techies' to an everyday medium for an ever-widening section of the population. The benefits it offers for the dissemination of information are clear, but can it now mature into a medium for mass communication and a major distribution channel?

Some senior marketers remain sceptical. The lack of objectivity and discrimination on the Web makes much of the information available worthless. They argue that while home shopping may successfully penetrate some product categories, in others consumers will continue to insist on scrutiny and inspection before purchasing the goods. Even if issues of privacy and security are addressed satisfactorily, users will remain reluctant to share all their personal details with Web operators who are not independent and trustworthy. Developing good quality interactive content is expensive, and what's more when it comes to entertainment, basic human psychology suggests that most people, most of the time, relax by being passive. Despite all the interactive opportunities on offer, the world's couch potatoes are unlikely to change their TV viewing habits overnight, and will continue to watch mass channels as long as they produce good quality programmes.

However, social, technological and economic factors suggest that the Internet's influence over our daily lives will continue to develop and change rapidly.

Access to digital technology is becoming the norm

In the 1930s, the average household had a wireless; in the 1960s most homes got a TV; in the 1990s it was common to have a PC at home; in the 2000s it will be 'normal' to have a digital receiver.

The UK government is committed to switching off analogue TV transmitters as soon as digital services are available and affordable, the criterion being when 95 per cent of homes have digital TV. It is predicted that this will be between the years 2006 and 2010.

New delivery systems influence behaviour

As access to the Web becomes easier, people are more likely to experiment with the many services it can offer. The advent of digital TV means that using Web-based services will no longer depend on having access to a PC. This liberates Internet usage from the office and study environment and brings the promise of a whole new experience in the living room. Interactive programmes, Internet access, games, services such as home shopping and home banking, will all be available from the comfort of an armchair. Viewers will eventually be able to access additional promotional information during commercial breaks by clicking on screen icons, which will take them to advertisers' Web sites.

The Internet is becoming an integral part of the economy

Society, in particular the business world, appears to have accepted the Internet as a new medium. This is reflected in economic life, as flagship firms invest billions not just into e-commerce but also the infrastructure needed to support it.

Technology promises 'ubiquitous connectivity'

As people become accustomed to using the Internet for everyday purposes, they increasingly demand both speed and continuity of access. It's no good relying on the Internet as a continuous source of information and 24-hour communication channel if you can only access it by dialling up from a PC or TV.

Broadband delivery through cable or high-speed telephone lines will not only provide good quality video, sound and animation but it is also fast and can be left permanently switched 'on'. With broadband there is no need to dial up a computer each time you want to check your mail or consult the Web for information.

Already we are promised Internet access on mobile phones and hand-held computers, with major players such as Microsoft and Ericsson teaming up to develop new software for the emerging mobile Internet market. This new portability will make it possible to rely on the Internet for information not just in the home and the office but also on the move. Industry analysts predict that more than 10 per cent of e-commerce will be conducted through mobile handsets by 2002.

Technology becomes more user-friendly

Intelligent agents are bits of software that start with a set of basic instructions and have the ability to learn. By learning their users' patterns of behaviour, they can anticipate their needs and become ever more personalized. The prospect of combining artificial intelligence with voice recognition technology opens up new possibilities. Imagine having such a personal computerized helper or 'avatar' represented visually on screen, who knows all your preferences, responds to your verbal commands, and searches the Web for suitable information, goods and services on your behalf. The more user-friendly the Web becomes, the wider its influence is likely to extend.

IMPLICATIONS FOR MARKETING

Marketing in an environment where consumers are empowered with near-perfect market information and are increasingly proactive provides a challenge. It will no longer be enough simply to broadcast or push the brand message to consumers. In order to survive in the Internet age, brands will need not only to establish a strong reputation but also offer good or added value, and be prepared to interact with users.

The new technology offers new possibilities to those with the skill and creativity to exploit it in a way that is relevant to users:

> We see this medium becoming ubiquitous, touching every consumer through multiple devices like mobile phones, personal organizers,

digital TVs and so on. This will give marketers who are truly committed to delivering solutions to the everyday needs of their target consumers the opportunity to respond more creatively, with products, services and even experiences that deliver added value. (M de Swaan Arons, marketing director, Unilever Interactive Brand Centre.)

The successful commercial exploitation of the Internet requires marketing specialists who are more than just 'technocrats' and who can find a way to exploit the technology of the Web in a creative way. There are great opportunities for marketing professionals who apply their skills and consumer insight to a new medium that has so far been technology-led and is still relatively under-developed commercially.

Useful Contacts and Further Reading

INFORMATION TECHNOLOGY

A glossary of computing and technical terms can be found on the Microsoft Web site (www.microsoft.com/support/glossary).

Whatis.com (www.whatis.com) has a comprehensive glossary of IT and marketing terminology for the Internet compiled from a variety of sources and contributions, plus discussions.

See Microsoft Web site (www.microsoft.com/smallbiz) for details of available software.

Macromedia's Web site (www.macromedia.com/shockwave) explains what the plug-ins Shockwave and Flash do, provides free downloads and technical support. It also links to sites that have successfully used the technology, a 'Shockwaved site of the day' and 'Flash gallery'.

For a quick and easy tutorial on the main technological principles behind the Internet and the World Wide Web, see Willy Wonka's Web site (www.wonka.com) and click on 'How it works' in the Wonkavision room. Aimed at kids, but great for big kids too!

For a much more grown up and in-depth study of the 'communications revolution' and how it affects the way we conduct our business and personal lives, see *The Death of Distance* by Frances Cairncross (Harvard Business School Press, www.hbsp.harvard.edu).

For a cynical view of the Internet industry, Michael Wolff's account in *Burn Rate* of how his Internet company went under has some interesting insights. See publisher Simon and Schuster's Web site for details (www.simonsays.com/burnrate).

CONSUMER RESEARCH

Forrester Research is a much-quoted independent research firm that analyses the future of technology change and its impact on business, consumers and society. It is US based, but has extended its Technographics segmentation model to Europe and opened an office in Holland. Subscription required (www.forrester. com/ER/marketing).

Jupiter Communications is a new media research firm that focuses exclusively on 'how the Internet and other technologies are changing traditional consumer industries'. Brief excerpts, samples and press releases are available on the Web site, but a subscription is required for any information of substance (www.jup.com).

NUA describes itself as an Internet strategy, research and development company and is based in Ireland. The NUA Internet Web site (www.nua.ie) provides statistics, charts and analysis on a range of different topics and markets. A lot of interesting data and leads provided at no cost.

NOP Research Group runs a household survey in Great Britain, and a children's panel (Kid.net) amongst many others. The Web site (www.nopres.co.uk) carries summaries of the key data and some analysis free of charge in the 'Internet surveys' section.

E-marketer provides statistics and demographic data on the Internet (www.e-land.com).

Datamonitor's new e-commerce service (www.datamonitor. com) promises 'in-depth consumer analysis and documented best practice to help you reach an optimal e-commerce solution for your company'.

For the latest new media stories, read *Marketing* and *Marketing Week* or visit their Web sites at www.marketing.haynet.com and www.marketing-week.co.uk.

Esomar is a Europe-wide group for market research professionals, and gives guidelines on market research on the Internet (www.esomar.nl).

Audit Bureau of Circulation (ABC) provides electronic and other media audit services (www.abc.org.uk).

Growing Up Digital by Don Tapscott (McGraw Hill, 1997) studies the generation that has grown up with computers, the Internet and digital technology. The associated Web site provides some insight and food for thought (www.growingupdigital.com).

PARENTAL ADVICE

Parents who seek independent advice about safety and security for children using computers can contact the Parents Information Network (www.pin-parents.com).

Recommended guidelines and filtering software can be found at a number of sites including: www.netnanny.com, www.surfwatch. com, www.rsac.org and www.cyberpatrol.com.

MARKETING STRATEGY

Many professional business advisers are deeply involved in developing Web strategies and e-commerce solutions for their clients, for example KPMG (www.kpmg.co.uk).

Competitive Advantage: Creating and sustaining superior performance by Michael E Porter (The Free Press, a division of Simon & Schuster, 1985, 1998). Introduces the concept of the value chain.

The One to One Future: Building relationships one customer at a time (Doubleday) and *Enterprise One to One: Tools for competing in the interactive age* (Doubleday) by Don Peppers and Martha Rogers (www.1to1.com), give a comprehensive and authoritative introduction to relationship marketing techniques.

Internet World™ Guide to One-to-one Web Marketing, by Cliff Allen, Deborah Kania and Beth Yaeckel (John Wiley & Sons) analyses one-to-one marketing strategy and technologies on the Web.

Integrated Marketing Communications, by Tom Brannan (Kogan Page, Marketing in Action Series) discusses the nature of integrated communication and gives a practical guide to planning and developing a strategy.

Creative Marketing Communications, by Daniel Yadin (Kogan Page, Marketing in Action Series) is a guide to planning, skills and techniques. It outlines the AIDA model for creating advertising and other useful principles.

TRAINING

I can offer introductory programmes for marketers, drawing on extensive experience of marketing fast-moving consumer goods, researching developments on the World Wide Web and diagnostic and training techniques. Individual and team programmes are available. For further details, send an e-mail to judy@iceco. demon.co.uk.

E-COMMERCE

The UK Web search 'Computers and the Internet' section of BT's electronic Yellow Pages (www.yell.co.uk) is a good start point for finding suppliers of e-commerce solutions.

Companies such as Intershop Communications develop and distribute e-commerce software (www.intershop.co.uk). Intershop provides shopfront software but leaves hosting to its partners such as Freecom.

For processing credit card payments, visit First Data Merchant Services (www.firstdata.com), or Datacash Payment Solutions (www.datacash.co.uk), which offer multi-currency services.

Freecom.net (www.freecom.net) offers hosted eCommerce Shops and Purchasing systems on a full service plan which includes adding the client's logo to a wide range of standard templates, and setting up departments, products, multi-currency VAT and multi-currency invoicing. Online credit card clearance is available subject to bank charges.

Shopcreator (www.shopcreator.com) is a Web hosting company serving other small businesses. For a one-off licensing fee, currently starting at £199, it will create or adapt an existing Web template into which clients drop price and product lists. Businesses then pay a monthly rental charge, which rises as the number of products featured on the site increases.

LEGAL

Data Protection Registrar www.dataprotection.gov.uk
Directive on Protection of
 Personal Data www.privacy.org
The Internet Assigned Names
 Authority (IANA) www.iana.com
The Internet Corporation for
 Assigned Names and Numbers www.icann.org
Network Solutions www.netsol.com
Nominet UK www.nic.uk

Registration companies providing search and registration services:

Register.com www.register.com
Netnames www.netnames.com

Glossary and Web Site Index

Access log A list of all the requests for individual files that people request from a Web site.

ADSL Asymmetrical digital subscriber line, a technology for bringing high-bandwith information to homes and small businesses over copper telephone lines.

Advertorial A brand-sponsored message and related editorial placed on an existing content site.

Agent *See* **Intelligent agent**.

Backbone The cables that carry Internet traffic. Backbones are like highways, except that they carry messages and files. Any message sent on the Internet, whether it's a request to see a Web page or an e-mail, goes first to the ISP, which then sends it into the backbone.

Bandwidth Measures the volume of information that can be passed along a communications link; in digital systems it is measured in bits-per-second (bps). A modem that works at 57,600 bps has twice the bandwidth of a modem working at 28,800 bps. It takes more bandwidth to download large sound files, computer programmes and animated videos to acceptable quality, than photographs or text.

Banner Advertisement placed on a Web site to flag information. Can be a simple message or moving images.

Bookmark Web sites can be stored as a 'bookmark' or favourite on the Web browser. This allows users to pay repeat visits simply by clicking the mouse on the selection.

Broadband A telecommunication that provides multiple channels of data over a single communication, for example through fibre-optic cables, which have a 'broad' or unlimited capacity to carry high memory media like video.

Brochureware   A term used to describe Web sites that are little more than online product brochures, ie, have few or no interactive elements.

Browser   The program that enables users to move around the World Wide Web by displaying text and graphics and creating hypertext connections. The browser is a graphic interface that hides the complexity of Internet navigation, and contains the basic software needed in order to find, retrieve, view and send information over the Internet. The first Web browser was called Mosaic, but Netscape Navigator (launched in 1994) is largely credited with transforming the World Wide Web and bringing the Internet into the home. At its peak, Netscape sold more than 80 per cent of all browsers, but by 1998 its market share was reduced to about 50 per cent, with Microsoft's Internet Explorer taking most of the other half.

Bulletin board   A host computer that is accessible by dial-up phone. Many bulletin board systems have Web sites, and many ISPs have bulletin board systems from which Internet users can download the software needed to get connected. Bulletin boards often offer chat and images for downloading.

Burn rate   The rate at which a new company spends its capital while waiting for the operation to become profitable.

Cache   When a user explores the Web, the browser keeps track of the pages visited and saves them on the hard disk so they will load faster when the user wants to return to them. This saves time and money because saved pages can be viewed without being connected to the Internet. Large networks such as America Online, ISPs, big companies, educational institutions and others store popular Web pages and then send them to viewers from the network's cache instead of repeating downloads across the Internet. This makes audience measurement difficult. For example, advertising placed in an electronic magazine can be viewed in three ways: on the original publisher's computer, or if the magazine has been cached on their ISP's computer, or the viewer's own computer. If they access it from the publisher's computer, the publisher will know how many times that advertising has been viewed.

Chat   Talking to other people who are using the Internet at the same time. These 'real-time' conversations are hosted by chat lines, chat rooms and forums. Participants type in text, which appears on the screen of other participants, who can respond. Chats are conducted on online services such as America Online, and some sites exist solely for the purpose of conducting chats (for example, Talk City).

Chat room   Where users can participate in a discussion by typing their contribution in on the keyboard. This is displayed within seconds on screen, and other users can respond. Some chat rooms are screened for inappropriate material, but many are left unsupervised, leading to some steamy and explicit contributions!

Click through   The number of users who click on a banner ad and visit the Web site it is promoting, as opposed to the number of users who simply see the banner ad.

Content   The ideas, concepts and formats that attract people to a Web site. The assertion that 'Content is king' is commonplace in Web circles, meaning that the information provided is even more important than the technology that delivers it.

Content site Term used to describe a site able to attract a large number of visitors simply through the utility of and interest in the information it provides.

Cookie A very small text file placed on a user's hard drive by a Web page server. It is essentially an identification card and can only be read by the server that placed it. The purpose of a cookie is to tell the server when a user returns to that Web page, so that the browser can recall personal details and registration for products or services, and show the information requested. Cookies only identify unique computers – as opposed to individuals – unless a user leaves personal information with their browser. Browsers can be set to accept or reject all cookies automatically, or to alert the user every time a cookie is offered.

Cybercafé A coffee shop or restaurant that offers access to PCs or other terminals that are connected to the Internet, usually for a per-hour or per-minute fee. Users are encouraged to buy food and drink while accessing the Internet.

Cyberspace A term invented by author William Gibson in *Neuromancer* to describe the place the players of video games imagined behind their screens. It has come to mean where people interact by means of connected computers, eg the Internet. Communication in cyberspace is independent of physical distance.

Data compression A way of reducing the amount of space or bandwidth needed to store or transmit a block of data.

Data mining The analysis of data for relationships. Information details supplied over the Net in digital format can be loaded into databases where software searches for similarities, differences and patterns to feed into marketing initiatives.

Data warehouse A database that can access all of a company's information. Data may be stored on several different computers in different databases, all of which the warehouse can retrieve and analyse.

Destination Web site A Web site that uses information, entertainment and production values to pull users in and generate repeat visits.

Dial-up A telephone connection to the Internet that is established and maintained for a limited duration, unlike a 'dedicated' connection, which is continuous or always 'on'.

Digital Digital information works on a single stream of ones and zeros, electrical positives and negatives, or pulses and lack-of-pulses. Computers have always handled information in digital form, but now information previously transmitted in analogue waves, such as music, speech and moving pictures, can be handled digitally. Once information is handled digitally it does not need a special machine for each task. It can be sent from one computer to another, or from a computer to the set-top box of a television. A personal computer connected by a modem to the telephone network can transmit video pictures and telephone conversations, although the quality may be poor. The same service can be delivered to the home or office by telephone line, cable or satellite.

Disintermediation   Cutting out the middleman.

Domain name   Every Web site and Internet address is given a domain name, as it is a lot easier for humans to remember a name than an IP address such as 217.165.135.170. An e-mail address usually consists of a name, followed by '@' (which means 'at'), and then a location ending in '.com', '.edu', '.net' or '.org'. Everything after the '@' is known as the domain name.

Download   Transfer a copy of a file from the Web to your computer.

E-commerce   Electronic commerce, or any means of doing business in an automated way.

E-mail   Electronic mail. Text messages and computer files exchanged between computers on the Internet.

E-tailing   Electronic retailing.

Encryption   The process of making data secure from unauthorized access on the Internet by substituting different characters for the actual characters. The code is then deciphered by the authorized recipient or processor. For example, credit card transactions over the Internet can be made secure by using **Secure Sockets Layer (SSL)** protocol or other applications compliant with the **Secure Electronic Transactions (SET)** specification.

Extranet   A closed network Internet for use between a company and a select group of external organizations.

Fibre-optic cable   A new type of cable made from ultra pure glass that uses lasers to transmit data at very high speeds and bandwidths.

Firewall   A security device to help protect a private network from Internet crackers and hackers.

Geek   Originally a circus term for a performer who bit off chickens' heads, adopted to refer to those Net users who spout technical jargon, acronyms and codes.

Hit   The number of times an item or file is downloaded from a Web page. When a user arrives at a new site and the site appears on the screen, every text and graphics file associated with that page is a hit. A page with five graphics and text would register six hits.

Home page   The opening screen of a Web site that welcomes the visitor and usually contains information on the content of the site, and an organizational structure.

Host   A computer with full Internet access.

Hotlink   A hyperlink that enables users to jump between Web pages or sites by clicking on underlined text, highlighted images or icons.

HTML (Hypertext Mark-up Language)   A set of instructions within a document that specify how it will appear on your computer screen when you view it on the World Wide Web or offline on your computer. HTML can also include references to still images, video and audio, as well as hyperlinks that enable users to jump between Web pages or sites by clicking on underlined text, highlighted images or icons. Also known as hotlinks.

Hypertext links   Enable Web users to jump from page to page by clicking on underlined text, highlighted images or icons. Also known as hotlinks.

Icon   A graphic image used to represent a topic or category of information on another Web page. Clicking on the icon may provide a hypertext link to that page.

Impression/ad view   *See* **Page impressions/views**.

Infomediary   An agent that uses information technology to gather, analyse and redistribute information.

Information superhighway   A term that has come to mean the Internet and its general infrastructure, including private networks, online services, etc.

Intelligent agent   A program that searches the Internet, gathers information on a specified subject and presents it to the user. Agents can be personalized or trained to adapt to their users' tastes and preferences. They include shopping robots, the Pointcast Network and URL-minder, which notifies you when specified Web pages have changed. Web search engines send out agents that crawl from one server to another, compiling the enormous list of URLs that form the basis of every search engine. An agent is sometimes called a bot (short for robot).

Interactivity   A two-way communication in which the Web user can participate. An active rather than passive experience.

Internet   An INTERnational NETwork of computers connecting millions of computers all around the world. Services on the Internet include the World Wide Web, e-mail and newsgroups, File Transfer Protocol (FTP), file download facility, and text-based bulletin boards. The Internet has its origins in 1969, when the US government decided to connect some of its computers together to enable scientists and military agencies to communicate more easily. The system was designed to be very robust, so there is no central control. Each machine operates independently and messages travel by whichever route seems most convenient at the time.

Internet Protocol (IP) address   A unique numeric identification for a specific Web site or Internet address. The Internet does not recognize word addresses, so name servers translate the URL into an IP address in order to locate the computer on which a Web site or domain name lives.

Internet Service Provider (ISP)   To gain access to the Internet you need an ISP, the company that routes your computer on to the Internet. When a user signs up with an ISP, a local phone number is assigned which the computer 'dials' into. Once the computer is connected to the ISP, the ISP switches the computer's connection directly out to the Internet network. Your personal computer can then communicate with other computers on the network. Early ISPs tended to charge a monthly subscription fee to cover access to cyberspace and services including a telephone help-line. In addition to the flat monthly fee, the user pays the telephone bill for time connected to the Internet. There are now over 200 'free' ISPs in the UK that charge no subscription fee, but the user still pays for telephone calls.

Interstitial advertisements   Advertising and promotional messages that appear without being requested on the screen as users wait for content to load, and then disappear automatically.

Intranet   A network designed for information processing within a company or organization. It can be used to distribute documents and software, give access to databases and training, track projects, etc.

Java   A programming language. The most widespread use of Java is in programming small applications, or 'applets', for the World Wide Web. **Java applets** are used to add multimedia effects and interactivity to Web pages, such as background music, real-time video displays, animations, calculators and interactive games. They may be activated automatically when a user views a page, or require some action on the part of the user, such as clicking on an icon in the Web page.

Knowledge management   A fashionable new term to describe the concept of deciding what information should and can be shared within an organization, and using technology to distribute that information. This often involves an intranet.

Micro site   A cluster of pages developed by a brand and hosted by a content site.

MP3 (MPEG Layer 3)   A way of compressing CD-quality music so that it can be downloaded over the Internet. To listen to the files you need an MP3 player such as RealPlayer's RealJukebox, or the latest versions of QuickTime or Microsoft Media Player.

One-to-one marketing   One-to-one or one-to-few communication with a customized message for each individual or narrowly targeted market. This contrasts with mass marketing where a common message is communicated to all.

Page impressions/views   Essentially the same thing as ad impressions/ views. The difference rests in a Web site's reporting of its traffic. If it has three ad banners on a certain page and that page is accessed 100 times, the site could honestly report 300 impressions (100 for each advertisement), but the page was only viewed 100 times.

Plug-in   Small piece of software that adds extra features to the browser, making the Web more interactive. Commonly used to display multimedia presentations in the main window, and access real-time data. Examples are Shockwave, which lets Web surfers play games embedded inside a Web page, RealMediaPlayer and Director, which enable the Web browser to execute animation, video and audio files, and Flash.

Portal   The point of entry to the Web. Also known as gateways, portals are typically ISPs and browsers that set their Web site as the default opening page for visitors, and search engines. The major portals are extending the services they offer in an attempt to encourage visitors to stay on their site as long as possible, and so attract advertising revenue.

Proxy server   A server that acts as an intermediary between a workstation and the Internet. Used by companies to ensure security and administrative control, and may also have a caching service.

Push Delivering a message to consumers instead of making them go and get it. Push technology includes e-mail, personal broadcast channels such as Pointcast, and intelligent agents that search the Web for specified information and take it to users.

Real time When something takes place live, such as a direct communication between two people, or a discussion forum.

Relationship marketing Developing a deeper understanding of the consumer through knowledge and experience. The consumer is the focus of marketing efforts, and communication becomes a dialogue through which loyalty can be built.

Search engine A service that indexes, organizes and often reviews Web sites. Different search engines work in different ways:

■ some rely on people to maintain a catalogue of Web sites or pages;
■ some use software to identify key information on sites across the Internet;
■ some combine both types of service.

No search engine keeps track of all content on the Internet. Even the major search engines – such as Excite, Infoseek, Lycos and Yahoo! – won't give you everything.

SET, Secure Electronic Transactions The specification encrypts data between a Web browser and a Web server, giving online buyers reassurance that their credit card details are safe.

Shopbot Shopping robot – a type of intelligent agent or software tool that compiles a database of products sold at online stores. The user gives a bot directions on what he or she wants to buy and it comes back with details such as prices and availability. Examples of shopping robots include BargainFinder, Shopguide, DealFinder and Shopfind.

Spam Automated e-mail or junk mail.

SSL, Secure Sockets Layer is a protocol for establishing a secure communications channel to prevent the interception of critical information such as credit card numbers. Used to enable secure electronic financial transactions on the Web.

Stickiness The qualities that induce visitors to remain at a Web site rather than move on to another site. Portals achieve stickiness first of all by having a great deal of content, but also by finding ways to involve the user with the site.

TCP/IP Protocol The network of computers that make up the Internet are connected to each other through use of a common standard protocol, TCP/IP. To establish a connection with another computer, a user needs to know its IP (Internet Protocol) Address. Since computers connected to the Internet can be of different types, communication between them is conducted through one of several pre-defined protocols. Most communication on the Internet nowadays is through FTP (File Transfer Protocol) and HTTP (Hypertext Transfer Protocol).

URL, Uniform Resource Locator The unique address of a Web site, consisting of the protocol, server or domain, and then a path and file name for individual pages. For example, http://www.unilever.com is the URL for the Unilever corporate Web site, in which http is the protocol and www. unilever.com is the server or domain name.

Users The number of people who visit a site. The log server records the number of unique IP addresses visiting a site, but this does not necessarily correlate with individual users. In order to count specific heads (ie, unique users) measurement software needs to be combined with registration information stored in databases or additional tracking technology, such as 'cookies'.

Viral marketing A new Web term used to describe any technique for getting users to spread the word about a Web site or service. When a site provides a solution to a consumer need that gets everybody talking about it, this is also known as **buzz marketing**.

Virtual mall A collection of transaction sites, often centred round online communities such as AOL. A merchant prepared to pay a fee, rent or commission on sales can access shopping trolley software and use the mall's central system for transactions.

Visits/User sessions A visit or user session refers to the activities of a unique Internet Protocol (IP) address during a determined period of time. For example, if a user enters a site and views four different pages, that person has logged numerous hits (four times the number of graphic files on each respective page) and four page views, but only one visit. If a user doesn't make a request for 30 minutes (if the site defines a visit as 30 minutes), the previous series of requests is considered a complete visit.

Web server A computer or programme permanently connected to the Internet, running special software that responds to commands from a client.

Webmaster/Webmistress The person responsible for creating and maintaining a Web site. Often responsible for responding to e-mail, ensuring the site is operating properly, creating and updating Web pages, and maintaining the overall structure and design of the site.

World Wide Web A service that makes use of the Internet. Based on three programmes: Hypertext Transfer Protocol (HTTP) is the standard format that enables computers to connect, exchange information and disconnect quickly. The Uniform Resource Locator (URL or Web address) is a standard method of addressing to enable networking computers to locate each other and make possible the hypertext linking from one site to another. Hypertext Mark-up Language (HTML) is the language that standardizes the way that Web sites or pages are created.

Web Site Index

Company	Chap.	www.	CONTENT 3rd party ads/ sponsorship	COMMUNITY access to info, chat, services/ shopping	PROMOTION marketing info for product/ service	TRANS-ACTION online sales	CORPORATE policy, investor relations, recruitment	BUS.-TO-BUS. info, e-commerce, industry bodies
Amazon Germany	3	amazon.de				x		
Amazon UK	3	amazon.co.uk				x		
Amazon US	1, 3	amazon.com				x		
America Online	6	aol.com	x		x			
Arcadia retail/ Principles	6	principles.co.uk	x			x		
Asda	8	asda.co.uk			x			x
Audit Bureau of Circulation	11	abc.org.uk			x		x	x
Avon	8	avon.com			x	x	x	
Bank of America	5	bankofamerica.com			x	x	x	
Barnes & Noble	3	barnesandnoble.com			x	x	x	
BBC	5	bbc.co.uk			x		x	
Bianca's Shack	6	bianca.com	x	x				
Bibendum	3	bibendum-wine.co.uk			x			
BMW	4	bmw.co.uk			x			
Boo	5	boo.com		x			x	
Boots the Chemist	4	boots.co.uk		x	x	x		
Cadbury Australia	4	cadbury.com.au			x			
Cadbury Canada	5	cadbury.chocolate.ca			x		x	
Cadbury Ireland	5	cadbury.ie			x			
Cadbury Learning Zone UK	5	cadburylearningzone.co.uk			x			
Cadbury New Zealand	5	cadbury.co.nz	x		x	x	x	
Cadbury Poland	5	cadbury.com.pl			x			
Cadbury UK	5	cadbury.co.uk			x		x	
Cadbury Yowie	4	yowie.co.uk			x			
Card 4 You	7	card4you.com	x	x				
Carling/Football Assoc.	4	fa-premier.com	x	x		x (merchandise)		

Company	Chap.	www.	CONTENT 3rd party ads/ sponsorship	COMMUNITY access to info, chat, services/ shopping	PROMOTION marketing info for product/ service	TRANS-ACTION online sales	CORPORATE policy, investor relations, recruitment	BUS.-TO-BUS. info, e-commerce, industry bodies
Carphone Warehouse	6	carphone.co.uk			x	x	x	
Charles Schwab	3	schwab.com			x	x	x	
Coca-Cola	7, 10	coca-cola.com/ coke.com			x		x	
CondeNast Health	9	phys.com	x	x	x			
Cosmetics Counter	8	cosmeticscounter.com			x	x		
Council of Internet Registrars	10	corenic.org						x
Data Protection	10	privacy.org						x
Dell Corporation	4	dell.com/euro.dell.com			x	x		x
Dunn & Bradstreet	1	dunandbrad.co.uk, dnbcorp.com			x	x		x
E-bay	3, 6	ebay.com	x	x	x	x	x	
Esomar	11	esomar.nl		x				x
FHM magazine	4	fhm.co.uk	x	x				
Financial Times	1	ft.com			x	x		
Fragrance Counter	8	FragranceCounter.com			x	x		
Freecom	8	freecom.net	x	x		x		x
Freemans	8	freemans.co.uk				x		
Freeserve	1	freeserve.com, .net, .co.uk, .org	x	x				
GeoCities	6	geocities.com	x	x				
Guardian/Observer	11	guardian.co.uk	x	x				
Handbag.com	2	handbag.com		x				
Hawkshead (Arcadia)	8	hawkshead.com	x		x	x		
HomeArts	2	homearts.com	x	x				
IBM	8, 10	ibm.com, uk.ibm.com			x	x	x	
ICANN	10	icann.org					x	x

Company	Chap.	www.	CONTENT 3rd party ads/ sponsorship	COMMUNITY access to info, chat, services/ shopping	PROMOTION marketing info for product/ service	TRANS- ACTION online sales	CORPORATE policy, investor relations, recruitment	BUS.-TO-BUS. info, e-commerce, industry bodies
Internet Ad. Bureau	9, 11	iab.net						x
Intershop	8	intershop.co.uk						x
Irn-bru	4	irn-bru.co.uk		x				
IVillageiVillage	2	iVillage.com	x	x				
Junkbusters	10	junkbusters.com						x
Lands End	8	landsend.com					x	x
Lets Buy It	3	letsbuyit.com				x		
Levi Strauss	6	levi.com				x		
Loaded magazine	4	uploaded.com	x	x	x			
Mapquest	1	mapquest.com	x	x	x			x
Mentadent tooth. Italy	5	mentadent.it			x			
Mentadent tooth. US	5, 6	mentadent.com			x			
Microsoft Small Business	7	microsoft.com/smallbiz			x			x
Mini	4	mini.co.uk			x			
MP3	1, 10	mp3.com	x	x	x	x		
Mum deodorant	4, 7	mum-online.co.uk		x	x			
Music maker	1	musicmaker.com	x			x		
National Westminster	3	natwest.co.uk			x	x	x	x
Nestlé	5	nestle.com					x	
Nestlé online shopping	8	le-shop.ch				x		
Nestlé Willy Wonka	4	wonka.com			x			
NetGrocer	8	netgrocer.com	x			x		
Netnames	10	netnames.com			x			
Nominet UK	10	nic.uk					x	x
NOP	2	nopres.co.uk			x		x	
NUA	2	nua.ie			x		x	x
Openmarket	8	openmarket.com			x			x
P&G Olean	6	olean.com			x			
Pampers	4	pampers.com			x			

Company	Chap.	www.	CONTENT 3rd party ads/ sponsorship	COMMUNITY access to info, chat, services/ shopping	PROMOTION marketing info for product/ service	TRANS-ACTION online sales	CORPORATE policy, investor relations, recruitment	BUS.-TO-BUS. info, e-commerce, industry bodies
Parent Soup	2	parentsoup.com	x	x				
Parent Time	6, 9	parenttime.com	x	x				
Peapod	8	peapod.com				x	x	
Pepsi-Cola	4, 7	pepsi.com			x			
		pepsi.co.uk			x			
Persil	4	persil.co.uk			x			
Pointcast/Entrypoint	9	pointcast.com			x			
Prince of Wales	2	princeofwales.gov.uk			x			
Pringles	4	pringles.com			x			
Procter & Gamble	5	pg.com					x	
Queen	2	royal.gov.uk			x		x	
QXL	3	qxl.com	x		x	x		
Racing Green	8	racinggreen.co.uk			x	x		
Ragu	7, 11	eat.com			x			
Register.com	10	register.com						x
Safeway	8	safeway.co.uk			x		x	
Sainsbury's	8	sainsburys.co.uk			x	x	x	
Tampax	4	tampax.com		x	x			
Tango	4	tango.co.uk			x			
Tesco	8	tesco.co.uk			x	x		
Time Warner Pathfinder	1, 6	pathfinder.com		x	x			
Unilever detergents, Eur.	5	clothes-care.com			x			
Virgin UK/online shop	8, 9	virgin.net/shopping	x	x				
Volkswagen Beetle	4	newbeetle.co.uk			x			
Wal-Mart	8	walmart.com				x		
Web Weddings	3	webwedding.co.uk	x	x	x			
Wedgwood	1	wedgwood.com			x	x		
Which?/Consumer Assoc.	8	which.net/webtrader		x				x
Women's Wire	2	women'swire.com		x				
Yellow Pages	1	yell.co.uk		x	x			x

Index